VIJAYANAGARA ORIGIN OF THE CITY AND THE EMPIRE

VIJAYANAGARA ORIGIN OF THE CITY AND THE EMPIRE

BY

N. VENKATA RAMANAYYA, M. A., Ph.D.,

Reader in India History and Archaeology, University of Madras

GYAN

Published by

GYAN

Gyan Publishing House
5, Ansari Road
Daryaganj, New Delhi-110002
Phone: 011-47034999, 9811692060
E-mail: books@gyanbooks.com

Distribution Network
gyanbooks.com
India, USA, Canada, UK, Australia, France

ISBN : 978-81-212-4556-2 (HB)
First Published, 1933

2nd Impression 2020

Printed at: Gyan Press, Delhi.

The book at your disposal is the edition of an old book originally published long back. The Text quality of this book may not be at par as compared to our other books but many readers approached us to reprint this important book so that it could satiate their hunger. We request all the readers of this book to help us to improve its quality by providing the necessary text of those pages which are not properly visible. Your valuable support in this case will be highly appreciated and acknowledged and our future readers will be benefitted immensely.

VIJAYANAGARA

ORIGIN OF THE CITY AND THE EMPIRE.

BY

N. VENKATA RAMANAYYA, M. A., Ph. D.,

Reader in Indian History and Archaeology,
University of Madras.

UNIVERSITY OF MADRAS.

1933.

PREFACE.

The following study is based exclusively on contemporary inscriptions and literature. The evidence of tradition is ignored more or less completely, as it leads to confusion and fruitless controversy.

I take this opportunity to thank the Syndicate of the Madras University for sanctioning the publication of this work. I offer my grateful thanks to Professor K. A. Nilakanta Sastri, M. A., for his valuable suggestions and criticisms, and to my esteemed friend Mr. C. R. Krishnamacharlu, B. A., the Superintendent of Epigraphy, Madras, for allowing me to consult the valuable collection of Telingāṇa inscriptions which he is editing for the Hyderabad Āndhra Research Society. I acknowledge with pleasure the assistance rendered by my friend Mr. A. Krishnamurti, M. A., who kindly checked the references and prepared the index.

"LIMBDI GARDENS,"
ROYAPETTAH, MADRAS,
9th December 1933.

N. V. R.

CONTENTS.

PART I.

PART II.

APPENDICES.

MAPS.

ABBREVIATIONS.

ASPP. ... Āndhra Sāhitya Pariṣad Patrika.

ASR. ... Report of the Archaeological Survey of India.

Beginnings. The Beginnings of the Kingdom of Vijayanagara by Father H. Heras.

Bom. Arch. Rep. ... Bombay Archaeological Report.

BSS. ... Bombay Sanskrit Series.

CHI. ... Cambridge History of India.

Des. Cat. San. Mss. Descriptive Catalogue of Sanskrit Manuscripts in the Government Oriental Manuscript Library, Madras.

Dyn. Kan. Dts. ... Dynasties of the Kanarese Districts by J. F. Fleet.

EC. ... Epigraphia Carnatica.

ED. ... History of India by Sir H. M. Elliot.

EI. ... Epigraphia Indica.

FE. ... A Forgotten Empire by R. Sewell.

Ferishta ... History of the Rise of the Muhammadan power in India by Muhammad Kasim Ferishta translated by J. Briggs.

HA. ... History of the Āndhras by Ch. Virabhadra Row.

HAI. ... Hindu Administrative Institutions by S. K. Aiyangar.

Historical Inscriptions. Historical Inscriptions of Southern India by R. Sewell.

IA.	...	Indian Antiquary.
JAHS.	...	Journal of the Āndhra Historical Society.
JIH.	...	Journal of Indian History.
JRAS.	...	Journal of the Royal Asiatic Society of Great Britain and Ireland.
Jr. Bom. His. Soc.		Journal of the Bombay Historical Society.
LA.	...	List of Antiquities by R. Sewell.
LR.	...	Local Records.
Mac. Mss.		Mackenzie Manuscripts.
MAR.	...	Mysore Archaeological Report.
MER.	...	Annual Reports of Epigraphy Madras.
Mysore and Coorg	...	Mysore and Coorg from the Inscriptions by Lewis Rice.
NDI.	...	Nellore District Inscriptions by Butterworth and Venugopala Chetty.
Num. Or.	...	Numismata Orientalia.
Pāṇḍyas	...	The Pāṇḍyan Kingdom by K.A.N. Sastri.
SII.	...	South Indian Inscriptions.
South. Ind. Muh. In.		South India and Her Muhammadan Invaders by S. K. Aiyangar.
Travels.	...	Travels of Ibn Battūta (Broadway Travellers).
VR.	...	The Inscriptions of the Madras Presidency by V. Rangacharya.
VV.	...	Velugōṭivāri Vamśāvaḷi.
VVC.	...	Velugōṭivāri Vamśacaritra.

PART I

THE ORIGIN OF THE CITY.

CHAPTER I

THE HOYSALA THEORY

Section 1:—An enquiry into the origin of Vijayanagara is essential for a correct understanding of the history of South India during the 14th century. The problem may be divided into two parts, viz., the origin of the city, and the foundation of the kingdom.

Who founded the city of Vijayanagara? It is not possible to offer a simple answer to the question, as it involves the discussion of a variety of topics which have apparently no connection with it. Several scholars hold that the city was founded by the Hoysala king, Ballāḷa III. One of them describes the origin of the city thus: "Various stories are related of the foundation of Vijayanagar. The fortification of the city that afterwards became Vijayanagar must, however, be regarded as the deliberate act of the great Hoysala ruler, Vīra Ballāḷa III. It was founded soon after the destruction of Kampili by the army of Muhammad, and immediatley following the invasion of the Hoysala capital Dwārasamudra."* In the opinion of another, the city was founded 'by a king who had been imprisoned by Delhi Mussalmans, taken as a prisoner to their northern capital, and then sent back to his country in the south.' 'Ballāḷa III was taken prisoner to Delhi, and afterwards was released by the Sultān. Hence Vīra Ballāḷa III seems to be . . . the founder of the city.' †

These statements are based on very slender evidence. The only source from which Ballāḷa III's connection with Vijayanagara is learnt, is a passage in the

* S. K. Iyengar *CHI.* iii p. 489.

† Heras : *The Beginnings*, pp. 41-43.

Rise of the Muhammadan Power by Ferishta where the foundation of the city is attributed to that monarch. "This year," (A.D. 1344), says he, "Krishn Naig, son of Luddar Dew, who lived near Wurungole, went privately to Bilal Dew, Raja of Carnatic, and told that he had heard the Muhammadans, who were now very numerous in the Deccan, had formed the design of extirpating all the Hindus and that it was therefore advisable to combine against them. Bilal Dew convened a meeting of his kinsmen, and resolved first to secure the forts of his country, and then to remove the seat of his government among the mountains. Krishn Naig promised, on his part also, when their plans were ripe, to raise all the Hindus of Wurungole and Tulingana, and put himself at their head. 'Bilal Dew, accordingly built a strong city upon the frontiers of his dominions, and called it after his son Beeja to which the word nuggar or city was added, so that it is now known by the name of Beejanuggar." *

The evidence of Ferishta, however, is not trustworthy, and it should not be taken into consideration; for,

(1) Ferishta records only a tradition written or oral which he obtained from some unknown source, when the city of Vijayanagara had already become a memory. Moreover, the story of the foundation, as it is narrated by Ferishta, contradicts the reliable evidence of contemporary documents.

(2) According to Ferishta, Krishn Naig's meeting with Bilal Dew took place in A.D. 1344. It is very much to be doubted whether there was any Ballāḷa alive on that date; for, the death of Ballāḷa III took place on Sept. 8, 1342; † and though his son, Ballāḷa IV

* Briggs: *Ferishta*, I, p. 427.

† *EC.* vi. Kd. 75.

ascended the throne on Aug. 11, 1343, * he did not rule long. Some believe that he ruled until 1346. † The belief is based on an epigraph dated in that year which is supposed to contain a reference to him. It records that in the year Vyaya a certain Jakkaṇṇa Nāyaka gave, to a Siddayāji Voḍeyar, Kāṭṭu-Nāyaka's Jaddapura during the time of Ballāḷarāya. ‡

Since the Śaka year is not given it cannot be definitely asserted that Ballāḷarāya of the inscription is Ballāḷa IV. There occurs a Vyaya in the reign of Ballāḷa II, and it is just possible that the Ballāḷa of the inscription may have to be identified with him. Secondly, the gift of Jaddapura appears to have been made some time before the grant was engraved upon stone, for the writer of the inscription alludes to the gift as having been made during the time of Ballāḷarāya. Assuming that Ballāḷa IV was alive in, A.D. 1346 it is just possible that he received Krishn Naig and promised to help him in overthrowing the power of the Muhammadans. In order, however, that he should be the founder of Vijayanagara, he should have had a son of the name of Vijaya or Beeja. There is absolutely no evidence to show that Ballāḷa IV had any children.

For the reasons mentioned above, it cannot be maintained, on the strength of Ferishta's evidence that Ballāḷa III was the founder of the city of Vijayanagara. A recent writer, in order probably to get over the difficulty, shifts the time of Krishn Naig's meeting with Bilal Dew to A. D. 1328. 'This date,' he declares, 'seems to coincide with the conquest of Warrangal by the Mussalmans, and the meeting of Kṛṣṇa Nāyaka with Ballāḷa III referred to by Ferishta.

* *EC.* vi. Cm. 105. † Rice : *Mysore and Coorg* p. 108.

‡ *EC.* ix. Bn. 120.

It was, therefore most likely at Tiruvaṇṇāmalai that the assembly of Ballāḷa III with his kinsmen in order to defend the empire against the Muhammadans was held." * To prove the correctness of the suggested date he cites an inscription : " One of the inscriptions that was most unfortunately overlooked ... is one that comes from Chitaldrug Talūka dated in the same year 1328. " It records that ' when the Hoysaṇa strong-armed Vīra Ballāḷa Dēva, together with the champion at his side, the strong-armed Bhīma Rāya, the prince Kaṭhōrahara, the prince Vīra Simha Raghunātha, the prince Kālamēgha, the Prince Vīra Śānta, Baiceya Daṇṇāyaka Camūpa who was the punisher of the famous Mādhava Rāya of Udēvara, the great minister Ballapa Daṇṇāyaka, the great minister Singeya Daṇṇāyaka were in the residence of the city of Uṇṇāmale ruling the kingdom in peace and wisdom. " " All this seems to point to the meeting of kinsmen convened by Ballāḷa III, as Ferishta mentions. It is interesting to notice that the place and the date of meeting are respectively Uṇṇāmale i. e., Tiruvaṇṇāmalai and 1328. Such are precisely the place and date of Ballāḷa's meeting with his kinsmen suggested in the above lecture. " †

The date of meeting suggested by the writer, it must be remembered, is not the same as that of Ferishta. He does not give any reason in support of the proposed change, except that his date, 1328 A.D. coincides with the conquest of Warrangal by Muhammadans. ‡. But that is not true, for the conquest of Warrangal was completed in A. D. 1323.

* Heras : *The Beginnings*, p. 122.

† *ibid* : pp. 124-125.

‡ *ibid* : p. 123.

Ulūgh Khān " entered the country of Tilang, took the fort of Bidar, and made its chief prisoner. From thence he proceeded to Arangal for the second time. He invested the mud fort, and after plying it for a few days with arrows from the *nāwaks*, and stones from the *mughribis*, he captured the whole place, Rai Laddar Deo, with all his *rais* and *mukaddims*, their wives and children, elephants and horses, fell into the hands of the victors ... The prince sent Laddar Deo Rai, of Arangal, with his elephants and treasures, relations and dependents to the Sultān under the charge of Malik Bedar, who had been created Kadar Khān and Khwāja Hāji, *nāib* of '*āriz-i-mamālik*. The name Arangal was changed to Sultānpūr and all the country of Tilang was conquered. Officers were appointed to manage the country, and one year's tribute was taken. The prince then marched towards Jājanagar, and there took forty elephants with which he returned to Tilang. These he sent to his father. * "

There is reason to believe that Pratāparudra was subsequently released and sent back to his country. He appears to have exercised some sort of control over a portion of his former kingdom until A.D. 1330. †

It is evident that the 'conquest of Warrangal' by Muhammadans took place not in A.D. 1328, as the writer under consideration would have us believe, but in 1323 A. D., five years earlier than the date of the alleged meeting of Ballāḷa III and his kinsmen. Therefore, there could not have been any connection between 'the conquest of Warrangal,' and the Tiruvaṇṇāmalai meeting. There is no indication that there was

* Barni : *ED.* iii pp. 233–234.

† *NDI.* ii Kr. 28.

a revolt and reconquest of the country between 1323 and 1336. In 1327 Muhammad bin Tughlak transferred his capital to Dēvagiri. Thence he sent an expedition against the Rāya of Kampili who offered shelter to Bahā-ud-Din Gushtāsp, the rebellious cousin of the Sultān. The Rāya was killed and 'the town was taken, its inhabitants were made prisoners.' Then the Sultān's army next proceeded against Bilal Dew under whom Bahā-ud-Din had now taken shelter and laid siege to his capital Dwārasamudra. Bilal Dew, however, submitted to the Sultān and surrendered the fugitive. These events took place late in 1327 or early in 1328. So long as the Sultān's armies were active in the South, there was no scope for the Hindus of Warrangal to rise up in rebellion. Tilang remained submissive for at least half a dozen years more ; for, no revolts broke out, and the Sultān could march to Warrangal and remain there without any trouble for some months in 1336 A. D. * According to Ferishta the meeting of Kṛṣṇa Nāyak with Ballāḷa III was followed more or less immediately by the expulsion of Muhammadans and the declaration of independence by Kṛṣṇa Nāyak; but all our authorities, contemporary as well as later, state that the expulsion of the Muhammadans from Tilang took place about A.D. 1345. It would not have been possible for the reasons mentioned for Kṛṣṇa Nāyak to confer with Ballāḷa III in 1328 for the purpose of overthrowing the authority of the Mussalmans.

Now, the inscription in which Ballāḷa III's meeting with his kinsmen is said to have been recorded, is very badly damaged, and some of the words cannot be made out. Mr. Rice, the editor of the inscription, remarks

* Barni: *ED.* iii. p. 234.

that "several of these names (occurring in it) are very doubtful owing to the inscription being indistinct." * Moreover, there is much difference between the printed Kannaḍa text and its transliteration :

ಹೊಯಿಸಣ ಭುಜಬಳಶ್ರೀವೀ
ರಬಲ್ಲಾಳರಾಯನೂ ಪಡೆಯೊಳೆ
ಗಂಡ ಭುಜಬಳಭೀಮ... ...ಯ.
ನರಸಿಂಹ...ರಾಯ ಶ್ರೀವೀರ...
ರಾಯಕುವರ ವೀರಶಂತರಾಯ
ಕುವರ... ...ವೀರ...ಗೆ ಖ್ಯಾತಿ
.........ಗಂಡ ಬೈಚಯ ದಂ
ಣಾಯಕಾಭ... ...ತು ಶ್ರೀಮ
ನ್ಮಹಾಪ್ರಧಾನಂ ಬಲ್ಲಪ್ಪದಂಣಾ
ಯಕರು ಸಿಂಗೆಯ ದಂಣಾಯ
ಕರುಂ ಉಂಣಾಮಲೆಯ ಪಟ್ಟ
ಣದ ನೆಲೆವೀಡಿನೊಳು ಸುಖಸಂ
ಕಥಾವಿನೋದದಿಂ ರಾಜ್ಯಂ ಗೆಯು
ತ್ತಮಿರಲು.

Hoyisaṇa-bhuja-baḷa Śrī-Vīra Ballāḷa Rāyanū eḍeyoḷe gaṇḍa bhuja - baḷa - Bhīma Rāyanū Kaṭhōra - Hara Rāyakuvara Simha Raghunātha - Rāyakuvara Kāḷamēgha Rāyakuvara Vīra Śānta Rāyakuvara . . . . Vīra . . . . Udavārada uṇḍige khyāti Mādhava Rāya gaṇḍa Baichayadaṇṇāyakābha . . . . Śrīman-mahā-pradhānam Ballappadaṇṇāyakaru Singeya daṇṇāyakarum Uṇṇāmaleya paṭṭaṇada nelevīḍinōḷu sukha sankathā vinōdadim - rājyaṁ geyuttamiralu &c.

The names:—

1. Paḍayoḷe gaṇḍa bhuja-baḷa-bhīma . . . ya.	1. Eḍeyoḷe gaṇḍa bhuja-baḷa Bhīma Rāya.
2. Narasimha . . . Rāya ...	2. Kaṭhōra Hara Rāya Kuvara.
3. Śrī Vīra . . . . . . Rāya Kuvara	3. S i m h a Raghunātha Rāya Kuvara.
4. Vīra Śanta Rāya Kuvara	4. Kāḷamēgha Rāya Kuvara.

* *EC.* xi p. 5 ; fn. to Cd. 4.

5. Vīra . . . ge khyāti . . . gaṇḍa Baicaya Daṇṇāyaka.	5. Vīra Śānta Rāya Kuvara.
6. Ballappa Daṇṇāyaka ...	6. Baichaya Daṇṇāyaka (Vīra Udavārada uṇḍige khyāti Mādhava-Rāya gaṇḍa.)
7. Singeya Daṇṇāyaka ...	7. Ballappa Daṇṇāyaka.
	8. Singeya Daṇṇāyaka.

Paḍayoḷe gaṇḍa bhuja-baḷa-Bhīma, Vīra Śānta Rāya Kuvara, Baicaya Daṇṇāyaka, Ballappa Daṇṇāyaka, and Singeya Daṇṇāyaka are common to the text and the transliteration, though it is more reasonable to take the first as a *biruda* than as a proper name. Nos. 2, 3 of the text are not found in the transliteration; nor Nos. 2, 3, 4 of the transliteration are to be seen in the text. The names, Kaṭhōra-Hara-Rāya-Kuvara, Simha-Raghunātha-Rāya Kuvara, Kāḷamēgha-Rāya-Kuvara, and Vīra Udavārada uṇḍige khyāti Mādhava-Rāya-gaṇḍa are added by the editor for reasons known only to himself. Therefore, these names appear to be fictitious, and they need not be taken into consideration. The only names which we can be certain of are those of Vīra Śānta-Rāya-Kuvara, Baicaya Daṇṇāyaka, Mahāpradhāna Ballappa Daṇṇāyaka, and Singeya Daṇṇāyaka. There is no reason to believe, in the light of the evidence before us, that these were the kinsmen of the king. The last two should not be confused with their famous namesakes, the sons of Ḍādi Sōmeya Daṇṇāyaka, for the name of their father is said to be Bēbeya in the present record. In 1328, Ballāḷa III was present at Tiruvaṇṇāmalai conducting a campaign against his southern neighbours. Naturally his officers were present in the camp with him. This had no connection either with the capture of Warrangal by the Muhammadans, or Kṛṣṇa Nāyaka's visit to Ballāḷa III.

(3) The members of the Hindu confederacy which expelled the Muhammadans from the South are said to be, according to Ferishta, Krishn Naig of Warrangal, Bilal Dew the ruler of Carnatic, the Rāyas of Dwārasamudra, and M'abar.

Ballāḷa III managed to hold his dominions intact until his death in 1342; and it is assumed that his son ruled for a short time without suffering any loss of territory. The capital of Ballāḷa IV was also probably Dwārasamudra, for the only inscription of his reign is found in the Cikmagalūr tālūka, in the neighbourhood of that city.* As Ferishta makes a clear distinction between Bilal Dew and the Rāya of Dwārasamudra, his information should be regarded as inaccurate.† Since at the time of the meeting it was the fourth Ballāḷa who had no children that was ruling, it is inconceivable how he could have named a city which he is said to have built after his son Beeja. The evidence of Ferishta should be regarded as incorrect and consequently untrustworthy.

It is asserted that Ballāḷa III was taken as a prisoner to Delhi in A.D. 1310, and was subsequently released somewhere about the commencement of A.D. 1313.‡ This statement is not based on evidence.

* *EC.* vi Cm. 105.

بلال دیو کشنا نایک را ملک داده از دو طرف رایان معبر و دہور سمند را که از قدیم الایام باجگزار
حاکم کرناٹک بودند۔

Tārikh-i-Ferishta p. 138.

‡ Heras: *The Beginnings*, p. 42.

Though the Muhammadan historians are not agreed among themselves regarding Ballāḷa's capture, they are unanimous in omitting to mention any prisoner of war. Amīr Khusrau who probably accompanied the army describes graphically the various incidents connected with the campaign, and he does not even remotely suggest the capture of Ballāḷa. On the contrary, a perusal of *Tārīkh-i-'Alai* leaves on the mind the impression that he was allowed to remain free. Barnī who was an younger contemporary of Khusrau states definitely that he fell into the hands of the Muhammadans; and Ferishta copies Barnī.

Though Barnī and Ferishta agree with each other regarding Ballāḷa III's capture, Khusrau does not even suggest its probability. As Ballāḷa III surrendered to the Muhammadans his wealth, kingdom and person as soon as they laid siege to his capital, there is no reason why he should have been made a prisoner. The source from which Barnī obtained his information is not known. However, his evidence cannot be lightly set aside as he was also a contemporary of Khusrau. Though it may be admitted for the sake of argument that Ballāḷa III was made a prisoner, there is no ground for the belief that he was taken to Delhi. On this point, all the three Muhammadan writers are in complete agreement. When Malik Kāfūr returned to Delhi in 1311 A. D., he is said to have presented to the Sultān the spoils of his southern campaigns. According to Khusrau, they consisted of elephants and gems: "The ground was covered by the large bodies of the elephants, and faultless gems." * Barnī describes the booty in greater detail: Malik Kāfūr presented to the Sultān 'six hundred and twelve elephants, ninety-six thousand *mans* of gold, several boxes of jewels and pearls, and twenty thousand horses.' † Ferishta reduces the number of elephants to three hundred and twelve, but with regard to the other items he repeats Barnī's account. ‡ None of these writers, however, mentions any prisoner of war. It is improbable that, had Ballāḷa III been taken to Delhi as prisoner and presented to the Sultān, this fact should have passed on unnoticed.

An examination of the inscriptions of the period (1310 to 1313) shows that Ballāḷa III was within his kingdom. He was ruling the earth together with

* *The Khasa'inul Futuh. JIH.* ix p. 78. † *ED.* iii p. 204.

‡ Brigg's *Ferishta*, i p. 374.

Mādigadēva Daṇṇāyaka and Aḷiya Māceya Daṇṇāyaka from Dōrasamudra in A. D. 1310 * In the next year, he granted lands of Belhaḷḷi to Harihara-bhaṭṭōpādhyāya, son of the *rājaguru* Viṣṇubhaṭṭa. † The inscriptions registering the gifts of some of his subordinates dated A. D. 1312 declare that Ballāḷa was ruling the earth in happiness. ‡ Therefore, it is not likely that Ballāḷa could have been absent from his kingdom. The inscription which is said to refer to his return from Delhi deserves to be examined in this connection. The person who returned from Delhi was not Ballāḷa III, but his son prince Ballāḷa Rāya, the future Ballāḷa IV. A perusal of the text of the inscription makes this point clear.

Svasti Śrīmat-Pratāpa Hoysaṇa Śrī Vīra Ballāḷa Dēvarasaru rājyamgeyuttimire Turuka Vigrayādalli ḍḍeḷi yanda makaḷu Vīra Ballāḷa Rāya Pataṇa *pravēśamādur*-avasaradalli Pramādi (śam)tsara Jyēṣṭha śuddha daśami yalli Kūḍaliya Rāmanāta Dēvarige dhārāpūrvvamāḍḍida dharma. §

The inscription registers a grant of taxes to god Rāmanādha Dēva of Kūḍali by Hoysaṇa Śrī Vīra Ballāḷa Dēvarasa in honour of the arrival of his son Vīra Ballāḷa Rāya from Delhi on 6th May 1313, after the Turuka war. The ruling Hoysala monarch in 1313 was Ballāḷa III; therefore, the Vīra Ballāḷa Dēvarasaru of the present inscription who made the gift, should be identified with him. It follows from this that he did not return from Delhi, but was in his capital. If Vīra Ballāḷa Rāya who returned from Delhi is identified with Ballāḷa III, then according to the inscription under

* *EC.* xi Cd. 1.

† *EC.* iv Kr. 43.

‡ *MAR.* 1907, p. 5; *EC.* x Sd. 36.

§ *EC.* vii Sh. 16.

consideration, his father's name should be Ballāḷa Dēvarasa. But the name of Ballāḷa III's father is Narasimha and not Ballāḷa. Therefore, the identification should be considered incorrect. If, on the other hand, Ballāḷa Rāya is identified with Prince Virūpākṣa Ballāḷa, the son of Ballāḷa III, this identification agrees with all the facts of the Hoysala pedigree and chronology. On the evidence of the present inscription, it cannot be asserted that Ballāḷa III was taken to Delhi as a prisoner by the Muhammadans and subsequently released. If imprisonment at Delhi and subsequent release should be taken as reasons for attributing to Ballāḷa III the foundation of Vijayanagara, it must be said that he had no connection with the building of that city.

The other grounds for believing that Ballāḷa III built the city of Vijayanagara are far less strong. No direct evidence, contemporary or later of any kind is available to maintain this view. It is based upon a series of indirect deductions drawn from half understood statements contained in a few inscriptions of the early Vijayanagara period, and may be stated in the following manner:

"There is an inscription in the temple at Hampi (known also as Virūpākṣam) referring itself to the Hoysalas, indicating thereby that Hampi was in the territory of the Hoysalas." Ballāḷa III "laid the foundations of the city generally called Hosappaṭṭaṇa or Virūpākṣapaṭṭaṇa." "There is further an inscription of A.D. 1354 (not at Hampe) which states that Bukka was ruling Hosapaṭṭaṇa." "In the next year, he is said to be in Vidyānagari, his capital." *

* S. K. Iyengar: *South India and her Muhammadan Invaders*, p. 172.

"This series of facts would put it beyond doubt that Hosapaṭṭaṇa and Vidyānagara are the same as Virūpākṣapaṭṭaṇa or Hampi and that this had been fortified against eventualities . . . by the Hoysala king Vīra Ballāḷa III." *

This view deserves to be examined closely. It is true that there is a Hoysala inscription at Hampe. In order to lend support to the statement that Ballāḷa III founded Vijayanagara, it should show that the region round Hampe was included in his dominions. The inscription, however, belongs to the reign of Vīra Sōmēśwara, and is dated in A. D. 1236, † exactly a century before the traditional date of founding the city of Vijayanagara. It does not help us to learn whether Hampe was included in the territories of Ballāḷa III. An analysis of the inscriptions during the period in the Beḷḷāry district may give us an idea of the people who held sway over it.

* S. K. Iyengar, *South India and her Muhammadan Invaders*, p. 171.

† *MAR* 1920, p. 33.

Ref.	Dynasty.	King.	Date A. D.	Place.	Tālūka.
M. E. R :—					
453 of 1914 ...	Hoysaḷa ...	Ballāḷa II ...	Nil	Sogi ...	Haḍagalli.
221 of 1918 ...	do ...	do ...	1180	Kuruvaṭṭi ...	Harpanahaḷḷi.
207 of 1918 ...	do ...	do ...	1185	Bennehaḷḷi ...	do
90 of 1904 ...	do ...	do ...	1194	Bāgaḷi ...	do
472 of 1914 ...	do ...	do ...	1194	Holal ...	Haḍagaḷḷi.
217 of 1918 ...	do ...	do ...	1195	Kuruvaṭṭi ...	Harpanahaḷḷi.
218 of 1918 ...	do ...	do ...	Nil	do ...	do
552 of 1915 ...	Yādava ..	Singhaṇa ...	1203	Pedakottaliki ...	Ādōni.
220 of 1918 ...	Hoysaḷa ...	Ballāḷa II ...	1205	Kuruvaṭṭi ..	Harpanahaḷḷi.
739 of 1922 ...	do ...	do ...	1205	Sandūr ...	Sandūr State.
123 of 1913 ...	do ...	do ...	1209	Magala ...	Haḍagalli.
124 of 1913 ..	do ...	do ...	Vikṛta	do ...	do
261 of 1918 ...	do ..	do ...	1210	Cigateri ...	Harpanahaḷḷi.
495 of 1914 ...	do ..	do ...	1211	Hirehaḍagalli ...	Haḍagalli.
126 of 1913 ...	do ...	do ...	1214	Magala ...	do
269 of 1918 ...	do ...	do ...	1214	Muttigi ...	Harpanahaḷḷi.
52 of 1904 ...	do ...	do ...	1218	Kuḍatani ...	Beḷḷāry.

Ref.	Dynasty.	King.	Date A. D.	Place.	Tālūka.
M. E. R :—					
743 of 1922 ...	Hoysala ...	Ballāḷa II ...	Bahu-dhānya	Talūru ...	Hōspēṭ.
68 of 1904 ...	do ...	do ...	Ānanda	Oruvāy ...	Beḷḷāry.
286 of 1925 ...	do ...	Narasimha II.	Nil	Hirehalu ...	Kuḍligi.
287 of 1925 ...	do ...	do ...	Nil	do ...	do
320 of 1925 ...	do ...	do ..	Viṣu 1221	Kottūr ...	do
38 of 1904 ...	do ...	do ...	1223	Kōgaḷi ...	Haḍagalli.
116 of 1913 ...	do ...	do ...	1223	Nilguṇḍa ...	Harpanahaḷḷi.
208 of 1918 ...	do ...	do ..	1223	Bennehaḷḷi ...	do
209 of 1918 ...	do ...	do ...	1223	do ...	do
281 of 1918 ...	do ...	do ..	1223	Anjigeri ...	do
280 of 1925 ...	do ...	do ..	1226	Bennikkal ...	Kuḍligi.
72 of 1904 ..	do ...	do ...	1228	Bāgaḷi ...	Harpanahaḷḷi
520 of 1915 ...	Yādava ...	Jaitugi ..	1229	China-Tumbuḷam ...	Ādōni.
LR Vol. 46 ...	Hoysala ...	Sōmēśvara ...	1236	Hampe ...	Hōspēṭ.
732 of 1919 ...	Yādava ...	Kannara ..	1254	Nagarūr ...	Ālūr.
733 of 1919 ...	do ..	do ...	1255	do ...	do
84 of 1904 ...	do ...	do ...	1251	Bāgaḷi ...	Harpanahaḷḷi.

525 of 1914 ...	do ..	do ...	1258 or 1259	Yenigi ...	do
488 of 1914 ...	do ...	Mahādēva ..	1262	Hyarda ...	Haḍagalli.
446 of 1914 ...	do ...	do ..	1263	Koṭnakallu ...	do
519 of 1914 ...	do ...	do ...	1264	Chimnahaḷḷi ...	do
33 of 1904 ...	Hoysala ...	Rāmanātha ..	1275	Kōgaḷi ...	do
34 of 1904 ...	do ...	do .	1276	do ...	do
480 of 1915 ...	Yādava ...	Rāmachandra	Nil	Sambukallu ...	Ādōni
717 of 1919 ...	do ...	do ...	1276	Neraniki ...	Ālūr
478 of 1915 ...	do ...	do ...	1278	Bassarakōḍu. ...	Ādōni.
243 of 1918 ...	do ...	do ...	1280	Kunchūru ...	Harpanahaḷḷi.
205 of 1918 ...	do ...	do ...	1281	Bennehaḷḷi ...	do
224 of 1918 ...	do ...	do ...	1282	Haluvagalu ...	do
486 of 1914	do ..	do ...	1283	Maila ...	Haḍagalli.
247 of 1918	do ...	do ...	1283	Kadati ...	Harpanahaḷḷi.
225 of 1918 ...	do ...	do ...	1286	Haluvagalu ...	do
242 of 1918 ...	do ..	do ...	1286	Kunchūru ...	do
718 of 1919 ...	do ...	do ...	1287	Neraniki ...	Ālūr.
248 of 1918 ...	do ...	do ..	1292	Kadati ...	Harpanahaḷḷi.
256 of 1918 ...	do ...	do ...	1297	Mannera Masalavada ...	do

The inscriptions of Ballāḷa II are found in Beḷḷāry, Hōspēṭ, Harpanahaḷḷi and Haḍagalli tālūkas as well as in the Sandūr state. His authority should have extended over these tālūkas, and probably also over Kuḍḷigi, as it was surrounded by his other possessions. The two eastern tālūkas, Ādōni and Ālūr, were governed by the Yādava king Singhaṇa. As Singhaṇa's inscriptions are also found in the Gooty and the Dharmāvaram tālūkas of the Anantapūr district, * it is not unreasonable to believe that Rāyadurg tālūka which lies between Ālūr and the Anantapūr district should have also come under his sway.

The successors of Ballāḷa II seem to have gradually lost their hold upon their territory in the Beḷḷāry district. The inscriptions of Narasimha II are found only in the three western tālūkas viz., Harpanahaḷḷi, Haḍagalli, and Kuḍḷigi. His authority seems to have been confined only to this area. Sōmēśvara is represented by a single inscription dated 1236 A. D., almost at the very commencement of his reign. He seems to have lost his hold on this region subsequent to this date. There is reason to believe that he was ejected from this district by Singhaṇa. One of Sōmēśvara's generals claims to have scattered the army of Kṛṣṇakandhāra; † and in an inscription dated A. D. 1237, "he is represented as first fighting against Kṛṣṇakandhāra." ‡ As Kandhāra did not ascend the throne until A. D. 1247, the events mentioned above should have taken place during Singhaṇa's reign. On the occasion of his war with Kṛṣṇakandhāra, Sōmēśvara seems to have penetrated as far north as Shōlāpūr, for an inscription of Sōmēśvara dated 1236 is

* *MER.* 345 of 1919; 298 of 1926.

† *MAR.* 1907 p. 4.

‡ *EC.* xi. Md. 122; *ibid.* iv. Ng. 99.

found at Pundharpūr. * Whatever be the cause of this campaign, Sōmēśvara never made any attempt to win back his possessions in the Beḷḷāry district subsequent to this date. Rāmanātha made an effort about A.D. 1275-76 to reconquer a portion of this region ; but he does not appear to have been successful. His Kōgaḷi inscriptions stand alone, and they remain the last indications of the Hoysala power in the district. It is interesting to note that neither Narasimha III, nor his son Ballāḷa III is represented by a single inscription anywhere in this region, though the rule of the latter was recognised in Kalyāṇadurg, Dharmāvaram, Penugoṇḍa and Hindūpūr tālūkas of the Anantapūr district in the neighbourhood. Therefore, it may be said that the Hoysala power in the Beḷḷāry district became practically extinct after the death of Narasimha II and that the Yādavas firmly established themselves in the place of their rivals.

Simultaneously with the disappearance of the Hoysalas, the Yādavas rose to prominence. They seem to have acquired not only the whole of the present Beḷḷāry district, but also Dāvaṇagere tālūka of Citaldrug district. Kṛṣṇakandhāra's rule over Ālūr, Harpanahaḷḷi as well as Dāvaṇagere is proved by his inscriptions in these respective areas. † Mahādēva's records are found in Haḍagalli and Dāvaṇagere. ‡ Mahādēva was an aggressive monarch ; he seems to have allied himself with the Cōḷa chief Irungōḷa Dēva II, and carried fire and sword to the very gates of Dōrasamudra. § The sway of Rāmachandra extended

* *Bombay Arch. Rep.* 1897-8.

† *MER.* 84 of 1904 ; 525 of 1914 ; 732, 733 of 1919 ; *EC.* xi ; Dg. 88, 103.

‡ *EC.* xi. Dg. 8, 87, 97, 100, 103, 162, 163, 171, 172.

§ *EC.* v. Bl. 120, 164, 167.

over Ādōni, Ālūr, Harpanahaḷḷi and Dāvaṇagere; and his authority seems to have been recognised in the other parts of this district. * The Yādava rule lasted in this region until probably the death of Rāmachandra in 1310 A. D. Power then passed into the hands of Vīra Kampila Dēva who ruled gloriously for a period of seventeen years. † In 1327, he was slain in a war with the Sultān of Delhi who annexed his dominions to the empire. This aspect of the question, however, will be fully dealt with in another context.

The inscriptions—if their evidence could be relied on—speak unequivocally that neither Narasimha III, nor his son, Ballāḷa III had anything to do with the Beḷḷāry district. It is therefore impossible that Hampe should have been included in the Hoysala dominions, during the reigns of Narasimha III and his son.

Section 2:—Hosapaṭṭaṇa.—Did Ballāḷa III build a city called Hosapaṭṭaṇa? Several scholars assert emphatically that he did. What are the grounds on which this assertion has been made? None. A careful search of the inscriptions of Ballāḷa III reveals the fact that they do not even remotely allude to Hosapaṭṭaṇa. It makes its appearance for the first time in the inscriptions of Bukka I, and nothing is known about it subsequent to the time of Harihara II. Though no evidence is available to attribute its construction to Ballāḷa III, it is necessary to locate the place in order to clear several misconceptions. Where was Hosapaṭṭaṇa? In an inscription of Citaldrug, dated A.D. 1355, it is stated that Bukka I was ruling from "Hosapaṭṭaṇa, the capital of Nijagaḷikaṭaka Rāya in the Hoysaṇa country." ‡ Two points must be noticed in this

* *EC.* xi. Dg. 13, 26, 59, 70, 81, Jl. 30.

† App. A. Note on Doravāde.

‡ *EC.* xi, Cd. 2.

context: (1) That Hosapaṭṭaṇa was the capital of a chief called Nijagaḷikaṭaka Rāya, and (2) that it was included in the Hoysaṇa country.

For the convenience of the present discussion the second point may be considered first. Where was the Hoysaṇa country? Sir Walter Elliot first identified Hosapaṭṭaṇa with the city of Vijayanagara.* His grounds for this identification are not known. As, according to tradition, Vijayanagara was newly built in A.D. 1336, and as Hosapaṭṭaṇa means 'new town', he probably considered that they were identical. Be his reasons what they may, his identification did not satisfy Mr. Lewis Rice, for Vijayanagara which is said to be identical with Hosapaṭṭaṇa "would not be in the Hoysaṇa country." † His objection, though legitimate, did not commend itself to later writers, one of whom brushes it aside with little ceremony. "It is beyond doubt," says he, "that the southern banks of the Tungabhadra formed part of the Hoysala Empire. One of the early Hoysala Emperors, Vinayāditya ‡ is called 'the ornamental head of the Kuntala dominion on the earth. It is therefore clear that the Kuntala country was within the Hoysala Empire from the early years of the dynasty. Now in the year 1430 an inscription of Dēva Rāya II testifies that the city of Vijayanagara is situated in the Kuntala country. Another inscription of Achyuta Rāya dated in 1538, similarly states that the city of Vidāyanagara (*sic*) 'belonged to the government of Kuntala dēśa.' The same is said in another inscription of Sadāśiva of the year 1555. Hence Vijayanagara

* *Num. or* 91.

† Rice. *EC.* ix, Intro. p 24.

‡ It is meaningless to attribute the term 'emperor' to Vinayāditya. He was only a subordinate of the Cāḷukyan kings of Kalyāṇi.

was also included in the Hoysala Empire, and could therefore be said to form part of the Hoysaṇa country. Consequently Hosapaṭṭaṇa may be the same as Vijayanagara." *

Considerable ambiguity lies hidden under the vague assertion that 'the southern banks of the Tungabhadra formed part of the Hoysala Empire.' It is true that the Tungabhadra was the northern boundary of the Hoysala kingdom in certain localities at times. The question, however, is whether it formed the northern boundary in the Beḷḷāry district during the reign of Ballāḷa III. The Hoysala power came to an end in this part of the country in A. D. 1275-76, when Vīra Rāmanātha probably made an attempt to recover what was lost by his father and half-brother. It is pretty certain that the country corresponding to the Beḷḷāry district was never included in Ballāḷa III's dominions. Consequently he could not have built Hosapaṭṭaṇa there.

The Hoysalas ruled over an extensive kingdom, but no evidence is available to show that all the territories over which they ruled were ever together known as the Hoysaṇa dēśa. It has been said that during the time of Vinayāditya, Kuntala formed part of the Hoysaṇa country. This is not true. On the contrary, the Hoysala inscriptions declare that the Hoysaṇa country was included in Kuntala. An inscription of the time of Narasimha II dated 1223 A. D., thus describes the position of the Hoysala country: "In the earth surrounded by the ocean is the Jambūdvīpa, in the middle of which is the Mēru, south of which is the pleasant Bhāratavarṣa. In it is the

* Heras: *The Beginnings*, pp. 56-57.

Kuntaladēśa, in which by nature a cow of plenty is the Hoysala nāḍ." *

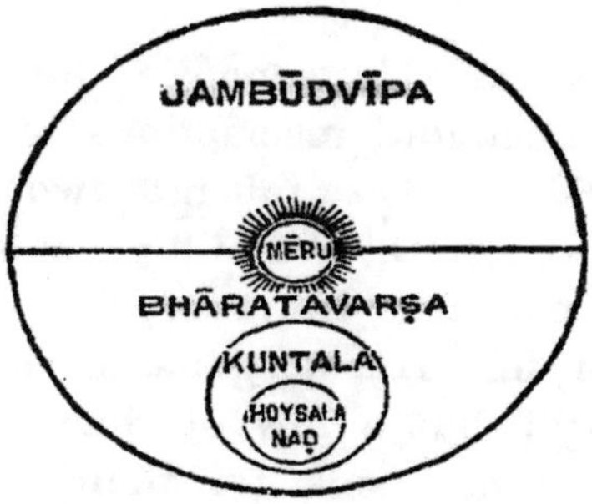

From this, it is clear that the Hoysaṇa country was but a part of Kuntala, and not the reverse. Moreover, the Hoysala kings used to distinguish the Hoysaṇa country from their other dominions, which they acquired by conquest: Narasimha III refers to his own capital Dōrasamudra where "he had established all the wealth of his own (*svakīya*) Hoysala maṇḍala." † He is said to have been residing in A. D. 1261, 'in his own Hoysala maṇḍala, in his proper capital Dōrasamudra." ‡ Ballāḷa III was "residing in his capital Dōrasamudra, in which his father had with affection stored the riches of a great kingdom." The capital is said to be included in 'his own Hoysala maṇḍala' (*svakīya Hoysala maṇḍalē*). § He was ruling in 1306 A. D. over "Hoysaṇa nāḍ, Konga nāḍ, and 18 other districts." ¶ It is obvious from these that the Hoysala monarchs applied the name Hoysaṇa nāḍ or maṇḍala to denote a particular part of their dominions which they specially regarded as their own. The Rāyas of Vijayanagara applied the names Hoysala nāḍ or Hoysala maṇḍala to the same

* *EC.* v. Cn. 197. † *EC.* v. Bl. 87. ‡ *ibid.* v. Bl. 74.

§ *MAR.* 1910 p. 20. ¶ *EC.* iv. Kr. 5; *MAR.* 1915, p. 56.

region. As the Hoysala maṇḍala was made a separate province of the new Vijayanagara kingdom, it was very often spoken of as Hoysala rājya also.

Where was this Hoysaṇa nāḍ or maṇḍala? In answering this question, inscriptions alone have to be taken as our guide. These fall into two classes. Some of them for instance CD. 2, and 3 refer to Hosapaṭṭaṇa in the Hoysaṇa country; however, they are not helpful either in identifying Hosapaṭṭaṇa or in locating the Hoysala country; but a few of them indicate places where we should not look for them. The so called 'Rāmānujāchāri edict'* mentions several places where the Jainas were to be found in large numbers during the reign of Bukka I. It refers to a petition of 'the Jainas of all the nāḍs within Ānegondi, Hosapaṭṭaṇa, Penugoṇḍe, and Kalyaha' to the Rāya. No useful purpose is served by proposing to identify Ānegondi with Hosapaṭṭaṇa, † for they are spoken of as two different places in the inscription. It may, however, be contended that Hosapaṭṭaṇa was Vijayanagara itself. Such an interpretation is not tenable for two reasons: (1) each of the four cities referred to in the inscription, appears to have had a few nāḍus under its jurisdiction. Ānegondi and Vijayanagara were included in the same sub-division of Hampe-Hastināvati and were regarded as a single city. Therefore, Hosapaṭṭaṇa which was at the head of a few nāḍus could not have been the same city as Vijayanagara. (2) Ānegondi is referred to in the inscription as a centre of the Jainas. Strangely enough not a single vestige of Jainism is to be found in the place; but on the southern bank of the Tungabhadra i. e., at Vijayanagara several Jaina

* *EC.* ix. Ma. 18.

† Heras: *The Beginnings*: pp. 127-128.

temples and inscriptions are still to be seen. In spite of the construction of Vijayanagara, Ānegondi or Hastināvati was still spoken of in the inscriptions of the time of Harihara I and Bukka I as their capital.* Ānegondi of the present inscription should be taken to mean Ānegondi including the new town, Vijayanagara, which could not have been very large at this time. Therefore, Hosapaṭṭaṇa and together with it Hoysaṇa dēśa should be looked for elsewhere.

Several inscriptions of the Hoysalas, the Rāyas of Vijayanagara as well as the Voḍeyars of Mysore register gifts of tax-free villages in the Hoysaṇa country to the gods and the Brāhmaṇas. They mention villages, nāḍus, and sīmes which can be located without much difficulty; and consequently they help us in identifying Hoysala nāḍ or maṇḍala. The table that is given below is bound to be useful in the enquiry.

* *EC.* viii. Sb. 375; *EC.* vi Kp. 6; *EC.* vii. Cl. 13.

Ref.	Dyn.	King.	Date.
EC. V. Cn. 197.	Hoysala ...	Narasimha II ...	1223
EC. V. Bl. 74.	do. ...	Narasimha III ...	1261
„ Bl. 87.	do. ...	do. ...	1265
EC. VI. Kd. 143.	do. ...	do. ...	1275
MAR. 1910 p. 20.	do. ...	Ballāḷa III ...	Nil
EC. IV. Kr. 5. also MAR. 1915 p. 57.	do. ...	do. ...	1306
EC. IV. Ch. 113.	Sangama ...	Bukka I ...	1368

Place.	Remarks.
Jambūdvīpa, Mēru, Bhāratavarṣa, Kuntala in which by nature a cow of plenty is the Hoysala nāḍ, Nirguṇḍa vṛtti in the Hoysala nāḍ.	The Nirguṇḍa vṛtti is to be identified with the tract of land surrounding Nirguṇḍa in the Hosadrug tālūka of the Citaldrug district.
The king was in his own Hoysala maṇḍala, in his proper capital Dōrasamudra.	Dōrasamudra is identified with Haḷebīḍu in the Bēlūr tālūka of the Hāssan district.
The king was in his own capital of Dōrasamudra, where he had established the wealth of his own Hoysala maṇḍala.	do.
The inscription mentions Āsandi nāḍ in Hoysaṇa nāḍ.	Āsandi is in the Kaḍūr tālūka of the Kaḍūr district.
It mentions Dōrasamudra in his own Hoysala maṇḍala.	Dōrasamudra is identified with Haḷēbīḍu in the Bēlūr tālūka of the Hāssan district.
It mentions the Mahāgaṇas .... and the chief men of Hoysaṇa nāḍ, Konga nāḍ and 18 other districts.	Since Konga nāḍ is equal to the present Arkalgūḍ tālūka in the Hāssan district, Hoysaṇa nāḍ should have been somewhere in the neighbourhood.
It refers to Gaṇapatima, governor of the south side of the Kāvēri in the country of **Viṣṇuvardhana Pratāpa Hoysala.**	**The Hoysala country should have extended at least in part to the south of the Kāvēri which flows through the Mysore district.**

Ref.	Dyn.	King.	Date.
EC. IV. Yd. 46.	Sangama ...	Harihara II ...	1376–7
MAR. 1915 pp. 57-58.	do. ...	do. ...	1377
MAR. 1913 p. 42.	do. ...	do. ...	1379
EC. V. Bl. 148.	do. ...	do. ...	1385

Place.	Remarks.
He made a grant of the village of Hebsūr belonging to the Kongu nāḍ on the bank of the Kāvēri in the Hoysaṇa country.	Hebsūr stands very near the Kāvēri. It is situated to the south of Nardanahaḷḷi in the Yeḍatore tālūka of the Mysore district.
It mentions Bāceyahaḷḷi belonging to the Kabahu district in the Hoysaṇa rājya.	Bāceyahaḷḷi is the same as agrahāra Bācahaḷḷi in the Kṛṣṇarājapēṭe tālūka of the Mysore district.
It mentions Sāgara situated on the Kapila in Bayanāḍ of the Hōsaṇa kingdom.	Bayanāḍ is identified with Heggaḍe Dēvanakōṭe tālūka. Sāgar is probably Saragūr on the banks of the Kabbina in the Nanjangūḍ tālūka of the Mysore district.
It mentions the village of Ghaṭṭadahaḷḷi in the Sīge nāḍ of the Hoysala kingdom.	The district cannot be located yet. Hn. 86 dated A. D. 1396 refers to Kaḍalūr- near Hāssan in Sīge nāḍ. In the Hāssan tālūka there is a place called Sīge Gudda ; probably the Sīge nāḍ of the present inscription may be tentatively regarded as the country in its neighbourhood.

Ref.	Dyn.	King.	Date.
EC. V. Hn. 36.	Sangama ...	Harihara II ..	1381
EC. V. Bl. 3.	do. ...	do. ..	1397
EC. III. Tn. 134.	do. ...	do. ...	1397
EC. IV. Ch. 114.	do. ...	do. ..	1398
EC. III. Sr. 89.	do. ...	Mallikārjuna ..	1458
MAR. 1914 p. 59.	Tuḷuva ...	Kṛṣṇarāya ..	1512
EC. V. Bl. 79.	do. ...	do. ...	1512

Place.	Remarks.
Singhapura situated in the Abalige nāḍ of the Hoysaṇa country.	Abalige nāḍ cannot be located yet.
It refers to Vēlānagari in the celebrated Hoysaṇa country.	Vēlānagar is modern Bēlūr, the headquarters of the tālūka of the same name in the Hāssan district.
It refers to the village of Hemmuge situated on the bank of the Kāvēri belonging to Tāyūr in the Pēre-ūr-country in the Hoysala kingdom.	Tāyūr is in the N. E. corner of the Nañjangūḍ tālūka on the Kabbiṇi very near its confluence with the Kāvēri.
Acaṇṇa Voḍeyar was governing the Hoysala country.	——
It mentions Mēlugōṭe in the Kuruvanka nāḍ veṇṭe of the Huyisala rājya.	Mēlugōṭe is in the extreme north of the Seringapatam tālūka in the Mysore district.
It refers to the village of Hiri-jaṭṭiga situated in the Vēlūr sīme of the Hoysala country.	Vēlūr is modern Bēlūr in the Hāssan district. Vēlūr sīme may roughly correspond to the present Bēlūr tālūka.
It refers to Kuppe, Mañcana-haḷḷi, Cikka-jaṭṭigahaḷḷi, Kādanka or Cinnādēvīpuram and Hiri-jaṭṭiga, belonging to Vēlūr sīme in the Hoysaṇa country.	do.

Ref.	Dyn.	King.	Date.
EC. III. Tn. 37.	Tuḷuva. ..	Kṛṣṇarāya. ...	1513
EC. V. H. N. 19.	do. ...	do. ...	1517
EC. V. Cn. 167.	do. ...	do. ...	1519
EC. III. Tn. 42.	do. ...	do. ...	1521
EC. IV. Kr. 11.	do. ...	Acyutarāya ...	1531

Place.	Remarks.
It mentions Mālānge in the Hadi nāḍ venthe on the south side of the Kāvēri in the Hoysaṇa country.	Hodināḍu or Nadināru is in the Nanjangūḍ tālūka to the north of the Kabbiṇi. Mālānge is Mālingi on the southern bank of the Kāvēri in the extreme south of the Turumalakuḍḷi - Narsipūr tālūka.
It mentions Narasiyapura sīme in the Hoysala nāḍ.	Narasiyapura is the same as Hoḷē-Narsipūr in the Hāssan district.
It refers to the village of Saṇaba which is situated in the Ātakūr sthala of the Hoysala nāḍ in the Ghanagiri kingdom.	Ātakūr is the same as Ātagūr in the N. E. of Mandya tālūka of the Mysore district.
It mentions Kalaūr in Mulūr sthala which was the Anantakṣētra, on the south side of the Gajāraṇya kṣētra which was southern Vāraṇāśi of the banks of the Kāvēri in the Hoysaṇa country.	Mulūr is the same as Mullūr on the south bank of the Kāvēri in the Koḷḷēgal tālūka of the Coimbatore district. Kala-ūr is identical with Kalaiyūr in the Tirumalakuḍli-Narsipūr tālūka of the Mysore district, very near Mullūr.
It refers to Belekere belonging to Sindhaghaṭṭa in the Hoysaṇa country.	Sindhaghaṭṭa is the same as Sindhughaṭṭa which is situated in the Kṛṣṇarājapēṭe tālūka of the Mysore district, in the neighbourhood of Mēlukōṭe.

Ref.	Dyn.	King.	Date.
EC. III. Md. 55.	Tuḷuva ...	Acyutarāya ...	1534
EC. VI. Kd. 158.	do. ...	do. ...	1541
EC. IV. Yd. 59.	Āravīḍu ...	Śrīranga I ...	1576
EC. III. Tn. 23.	Mysore ...	Dēvarāja II ...	1663
EC. IV. Kr. 67.	do. ...	do. ...	1663

Place.	Remarks.
It mentions Māragoṇḍanahaḷḷi situated on the banks of the Kāvēri in the great Hoysala nāḍ in the Śrīrangapaṭṭaṇa country.	Śrīrangapaṭṭaṇa is Seringapatam on the Kāvēri in the Mysore district.
It refers to Muktihaḷḷi, Hiriyūr and other villages in the Āsandi nāḍ in the Yakaṭṭi sīme in the Hoysala nāḍ of the Southern country.	Āsandi is in the extreme north of the Kaḍūr tālūka of the same district. The villages must be somewhere in the neighbourhood of Āsandi.
It records the grant of Rāmapura in the Hampāpura sthala belonging to the Narasimhapura sīme, situated in the middle of the Kāvēri in the Hoysaṇa kingdom.	Hampāpura is in the Yeḍatore tālūka of the Mysore district on the Kāvēri near its confluence with the Hēmāvati. Narasimhapura is the same as Hoḷē-Narsipūr in the Kaḍūr district.
It refers to Haḷḷikere situated in the Nāgamangaḷa sthala in the Hoysala nāḍ.	Nāgamangaḷa is the headquarters of the tālūka of the same name in the Mysore district.
It records the grant of Māḷagūr belonging to Bācahaḷḷi sthala in the western Nāgamangaḷa hōbaḷi in the Hoysala nāḍ.	Bācahaḷḷi is identical with agrahāra-Bācēhaḷḷi in the Kṛṣṇarājapēṭe tālūka of the Mysore district.

Ref.	Dyn.	King.	Date.
EC. IV. Yd. 54.	Mysore ...	Dēvarāja II ...	1666
Yd. 53 ...	do. ...	do. ...	1666
Yd. 43 ...	do. ...	do. ...	1667

Place.	Remarks.
It refers to the village of Bhēriya in the neighbourhood of Narasimhanagara in the Hoysala nāḍ country.	The village of Bhēriya is in the north of Yeḍatore tālūka in the neighbourhood of Akkihabal in the Kṛṣṇarājapēṭe tālūka of the Mysore district.
It mentions the village of Bhērya belonging to Narasimhapura in the middle of the Kāvēri in the Hoysaṇa country.	The village of Bhērya is different from Bhēriya as the former is said to be in the middle of the Kāvēri. Narasimhapura is, no doubt, Hoḷē-Narsipūr.
Sālagrama belonging to Narasimhapura in the Hoysaṇa nāḍ country.	Sālagrama is in the Yeḍatore tālūka of the Mysore district. Narasimhapura is Hoḷē-Narsipūr.

The thirty one inscriptions examined in this connection belong to five dynasties (the Hoysala, the Sangama, the Tuḷuva, the Āravīḍu and the Mysore) ranging from A. D. 1223 to 1667. During this long period of nearly 450 years, the name Hoysala nāḍ, maṇḍala, dēśa, or rājya was made use of to denote a tract of territory included in the present Mysore state. All the villages or the districts to which they belonged are found in Mysore, Hāssan, and Kaḍūr districts. In the east, the Hoysala nāḍ appears to have extended to the borders of the Bangalore district and in the south, it included the Koḷḷēgal tālūka of the Coimbatore district. Therefore, the Hoysaṇa nāḍ, maṇḍala, dēśa, or rājya denoted a tract of country, well within the boundaries of the present Mysore state. A search should be made in this region for Hosapaṭṭaṇa, a city which rose to prominence during the days of the early Sangamas. The two inscriptions from Citaldrug (Cd. 2, 3) state that Bukka I was ruling from Hosapaṭṭaṇa in the Hoysaṇadēśa. In another inscription he is represented as ruling from Penugoṇḍe and Hosapaṭṭaṇa. * And in an undated epigraph of his reign found at Sakrepaṭṭaṇa in the Kaḍūr district, Hosapaṭṭaṇa is described, as "the face of the goddess of the Hoysala kingdom, and a mirror of the goddess of the kingdom of Vīra Bukka." † It appears from this that Hosapaṭṭaṇa was the capital of the Hoysala country during the reign of Bukka I.

Where was Hosapaṭṭaṇa situated in the Hoysala country? While looking for the place, the following points may usefully be remembered:

(1) It should be in the Hoysala country.

* *MER.* 522 of 1906.

† *MAR.* 1927 No. 48, p. 61.

(2) It should be situated in a region where the Jainas and the Vaiṣṇavas could have come into conflict.

(3) It should be in the neighbourhood of the fort of Nijagaḷi whose lord it could have served as a capital at one time.

(4) These are essential; and if, in addition to these, it has the name of Hosapaṭṭaṇa, the problem may be considered as solved finally.

Commenting on the Sakrepaṭṭaṇa epigraph, Dr. Ṣāma Śāstri observes, "The present record would tend to show that Hosapaṭṭaṇa was either the village of Sakrepaṭṭaṇa, where the present inscription stone is found or some village in the neighbourhood." * Speaking of another inscription at Hosavūr he declares, "Hosavūr may probably be the same as Hosapaṭṭaṇa." † This identification satisfies almost all the conditions laid down above, though neither of the places suggested by Dr. Ṣāma Śāstri bears the name of Hosapaṭṭaṇa. Hosapaṭṭaṇa is neither Sakrepaṭṭaṇa nor Hosavūr, but it stands at some distance from them on an island in the Hēmāvati river in the Kṛṣṇarāja-pēṭe tālūka of the Mysore district. At present, 'an anicut in two sections' is built 'abutting on the island of Hosapaṭṭaṇa where there is an old deserted fort.' ‡ Having thus spotted Hosapaṭṭaṇa, it is necessary to find out whether this place satisfies the above mentioned conditions.

(1) Its name is Hosapaṭṭaṇa.

(2) It stands in the neighbourhood of Śrāvaṇa-Beḷgoḷa in the Cannarāyapaṭṭaṇa tālūka of the

* *MAR.* 1927 p. 62. † *ibid.* p. 63.

‡ Rice, *Mysore Gazetteer* Vol. ii. p. 250.

Hāssan district (16 miles), a Jaina centre, and of Mēlukōṭe (17 miles) in the Kṛṣṇarājapēṭe tālūka of the Mysore district, a Vaiṣṇava centre. It is known that the Jainas and the Vaiṣṇavas would come, on occasions, into conflict.

(3) It is in the very heart of the Hoysala country. The village of Bheriya which, according to an inscription of 1666 (Yd. 54), was included in the Hoysala country, stands in the immediate neighbourhood of Hosapaṭṭaṇa.

(4) Nijagaḷi kaṭaka rāya or the chief of the fort of Nijagaḷi is mentioned in one of the Western Ganga records. He was a Cāḷukyan prince, and his daughter Jākāmbā was given in marriage to the Ganga king, Eṟeganga-Dēva-Nītimārga. * It is evident from this that the lord of the fort of Nijagaḷi lived a few centuries before the foundation of the city of Vijayanagara. Since Hosapaṭṭaṇa was his capital, it should have been in existence from his time. The village of Nijagaḷi, which gave the chief his name, can also be located. Nijagaḷi is in the Hoysala country. It is situated in the Nelamangaḷa tālūka of the Bangalore district where it touches the frontiers of Tumkūr.

Therefore, the identity of Hosapaṭṭaṇa may be taken to have been finally established.

Section 3 :— Virūpākṣapura. — Virūpākṣapura or Virūpākṣapaṭṭaṇa which is mentioned in Ballāḷa III's

* *MAR*. 1921, pp. 11, 21, 25.

Vṛtta :—

Tasya brahma-mahīndra-bṛnda-makuṭa-vyāsakta-raktātuḷa
Cchāyā-kuṅkuma-mañjarīkṛta-pada-dvandvasya dēvyām prabhuḥ
Cāḷukyāmaḷa-vamśa-bhū-*Nijagaḷi-kṣmāpāḷa* putryām abhur
Jyākāmbā-vyapadēśa-bhāji tanayaḥ Śrī Satyavākyō nṛpaḥ. ||

inscriptions as one of his *nelevīḍus* is identified with Hampe, and consequently with Vijayanagara. It is stated that "Vīra Ballāḷa III was the real founder of the city of Vīra - Vijaya - Virūpākṣapura, which eventually became Vijayanagar not long after." * "Śrī - Vīra - Vijaya - Virūpākṣapura was the city of Vijayanagara." "It was called first Vijaya. But besides, the city bore the name of Śrī-Vīra-Virūpākṣa, that is exactly the name of Vīra Ballāḷa III's son." † "The full name of Vīra Ballāḷa III's son was most likely Śrī-Vīra-Vijaya-Virūpākṣa." ‡

The following propositions emerge from these statements.

(i) Ballāḷa III had a son called Vīra-Vijaya-Virūpākṣa Ballāḷa.

(ii) He built a city called Vīra-Vijaya-Virūpākṣapura, evidently naming it after his son.

(iii) Vīra-Vijaya-Virūpākṣapura was also known as Hampe which formed a single city with Vijayanagara. Therefore, Vīra - Vijaya - Virūpākṣapura is identical with Vijayanagara.

(i) There is no contemporary evidence to show that the word "Vijaya" formed part of the name of Virūpākṣa Ballāḷa. No doubt, it occurs in the name, Śrī - Vijaya - Virūpākṣapura; but there is nothing to connect the name of the village with that of the prince. The term 'Vijaya' seems to be prefixed sometimes to the names of certain villages in the inscriptions; *e. g.*, the village of Araseyakere was known as Vīra-Vijaya-

* Heras : *The Beginnings*, p. 55.

† *ibid* : p. 46.

‡ *ibid* : p. 45. n. 2.

Ballāḷapura. * In cases such as these 'Vijaya' should be taken as an honorific epithet qualifying the name of the village, and not as a proper name denoting a person.

(ii) Again, there is no indication in his numerous inscriptions that Ballāḷa III had ever built any town or fort. The Hoysala monarchs seem to take some pleasure in mentioning the places which they built or improved. Sōmēśwara is said to have built Vikramapura † and Vijayarājēndrapaṭṭaṇa. ‡ Narasimha III improved the condition of Dōrasamudra 'by storing in it' all the wealth of his own Hoysala kingdom. § Ballāḷa III had rebuilt the capital after it had been destroyed by the attack of the Muhammadans in 1310 A. D. ¶ Some of his officers made Caṇḍināyakanahaḷḷi into a paṭṭaṇa in A. D. 1319. || It is strange that no mention of the construction of a town called Vīra-Vijaya-Virūpākṣapura by Ballāḷa III is made in his inscriptions.

(iii) Hampe was occasionally spoken of as Virūpākṣam; ** and so far as I am aware, this name was specially associated with the Adwaita *maṭha* in the place. It had never been used to denote the town or the village surrounding the temple. Granting that the

* *EC.* v. Ak. 72. See also Ak. 49, and 50 dated A.D. 1215 and 1227 respectively. They refer to an agrahāra called Vijaya-Narasimhapura. The agrahāra was probably granted either by or for the religious merit of Narasimha II. There is no evidence to show that Narasimha II had the name of Vijaya. The word 'Vijaya' in cases such as these, should be interpreted as an epithet qualifying the name which it precedes. Vijaya-Virūpākṣapura belongs to the same class of names as Vijaya-Vaijayanti, Vijaya-Vengīpura, Vijaya-Daśanapura etc.

† *EC.* ix. Bn. 6.

‡ *MAR.* 1913. Two inscriptions at Ellespūr.

§ *EC.* v. Bl. 74, 87.

¶ *EC.* iii. Md. 100.

|| *EC.* ix. Cp. 12.

** *MAR.* 1916, p. 95, 96.

name denoted the town also, no evidence is forthcoming to connect Ballāḷa III's name with it. It has already been shown that the Beḷḷāry district in which Hampe is situated was never included in the dominions of Ballāḷa III or that of his father. This region passed in 1328 A. D. into the hands of the Sultān of Delhi who attacked Ballāḷa, and forced him to pay tribute. Under these circumstances, it is not possible that Ballāḷa could have founded a town in a place which was included in the dominions of his enemy, the Sultān of Delhi. Therefore, a search should be made for Virūpākṣapura within the dominions of Ballāḷa III.

Three places bearing the name Virūpākṣapura are found within the kingdom of Ballāḷa III. One of them is mentioned in an inscription of Mulbāgal dated 1431 A.D. * Another is found in the Cannapaṭṭaṇa tālūka of the Bangalore district; and a third is referred to in an inscription of Paduvari, in the Coondāpoor tālūka of the South Canara district, dated A. D. 1360. † Ballāḷa III might have been residing in any one of these places. However, none of these should be identified with Virūpākṣapura mentioned in his inscriptions. There is a place in the Magdi tālūka of the Bangalore district called Virūpapura, where we find several inscriptions of Ballāḷa III and his subordinates. ‡ Now, Virūpapura, is obviously an abbreviated form of Virūpākṣapura. It appears to have been a resort frequently visited by Ballāḷa, owing probably to the presence in the place of a renowned Śaivite teacher called Gurucittadēva. § It is reasonable to think that Virūpapura is identical with the Virūpākṣapura or paṭṭaṇa of Ballāḷa III's inscriptions, and that it has no connection whatever with Hampe-Virūpākṣam.

* *EC.* x. Mb. 2.

† *MER.* 546 of 1930.

‡ *MAR.* 1915 p. 56.

§ *ibid.*

Section 4 :—Hosa-Hampeya Paṭṭaṇa.—This place, which is said to be mentioned in one of the inscriptions of Harihara I dated A. D. 1340, is identified with Vijayanagara. "In the time of Harihara," says a recent writer, "Vijayanagara was popularly known as Hosa-Hampeya Paṭṭaṇa." *

The inscription from which the above information is derived comes from Kundurpi in the Kalyāṇadurg tālūka of the Anantapūr district. † It has absolutely no connection with Harihara I; his name or the name of anyone else who is connected with him is not even remotely alluded to in it. It is a record, as the epigraphist correctly observes, 'of the Hoysala king Vīra Ballāḷa, the son of Vīra Narasinga, who had his headquarters in Dōrasamudra.' 'It mentions a Mahāsāmanta of the king by name Bommeya Nāyaka, son of Gangeya Nāyaka who was governing the Niḍugal rājya, and mentions Hosa-Hampeya Paṭṭaṇa.' From this, it is evident that Harihara I had nothing to do with the present inscription.

The identification of Hosa-Hampeya Paṭṭaṇa with Hampe is not tenable. Hosa-Hampeya Paṭṭana means the town of New Hampe, and it should have been so named for distinguishing it from Old Hampe. Just as New york and New Jersey cannot be the same towns as York and Jersey, so New Hampe cannot be identical with the old town of Hampe. Hosa-Hampeya Paṭṭaṇa seems to have been included in the Niḍugal rājya which Mahāsāmanta Bommeya Nāyaka, a subordinate of Ballāḷa III was ruling in 1340 A.D. It must be noted that the inscriptions of Ballāḷa III or of his subordinates are found only in the Anantapūr district.

* Heras: *The Beginnings*, p. 58.

† *MER.* 102 of 1927.

And not one of them is to be found anywhere in Beḷḷāry. Hosa-Hampeya Paṭṭaṇa, therefore, should be looked for within Ballāḷa's dominions and not without. In the Anantapūr tālūka, there is a village called Hampāpuram with which Hosa-Hampeya Paṭṭaṇa may provisionally be identified. The authority of Bommeya Nāyaka, could not have extended to Hampe in 1340, for Harihara I was already ruling from that place at that time. It cannot be said that Harihara was a subordinate of Bommeya Nāyaka; for, what little evidence we have at our command goes against the supposition. At the present state of our knowledge, we are justified only in holding that there was a place in Ballāḷa's dominions called Hosa-Hampeya Paṭṭaṇa whose identity cannot yet be fully established.

CHAPTER II.

THE FOUNDERS OF VIJAYANAGARA

Section 1.—Who founded Vijayanagara? A few inscriptions of the early kings of Vijayanagara describe the manner in which the city was founded. Two copper-plate grants both dated in 1336 A.D., attribute the foundation of the city to Harihara I.

It is said in the Kāpalūr grant that on one occasion king Harihara who was ruling at Kuñjarakōna, on the Tungabhadra, after crossing that river went out hunting in the forest on the southern bank. There he was astonished to see a hound being bitten by a hare. "He went to the hermit Vidyāraṇya, the incarnation of spiritual knowledge, whose austerity was honoured and who was like another Mahēśāna (Śiva), who (resided) near his (Virūpākṣa's) temple. Having saluted in his vicinity with reverence ...... he related this incident whose explanation was wonderful." Vidyāraṇya, the best of the ascetics said: "O king, the country deserves to be the residence of a family of great kings, and the sole source of great power! Oh Lord, found a city named Vidyā." "Having accordingly obeyed his command, occupying the seat of kings (throne), conspicuous with an excellent white umbrella, having indeed performed gifts which were even greater than the sixteen gifts, he, king Harihara shone in the extensive town named Vidyā." *

The same story is narrated in another grant of the same date. King Harihara who ruled at Kuñjarakōna,

* *NDI.* Vol. i. Cp. No. 15.

on one occasion " crossed the Tungabhadra with the intention of hunting, and coming forth with his army, saw the forest to the South. And in that forest, that moon to the ocean of Sangamēśa was surprised to see a fierce dog with long teeth, only chewing what had been bitten, and a hare. And seeing the God Virūpākṣa along with the Goddess Pampā, he did obeisance to them, and drawing near the *yati* in that temple, informed him of the above curious circumstance." Vidyāraṇya said, 'O king, this place is worthy to be the residence of a family of great kings ; this is a specially strong site. Make here a city named Vidyā.' Thereupon Hariharēśvara, doing according to his direction, was seated on the throne, and adorned with the white umbrella, made the sixteen great gifts resplendent in the *nagara* called Vidyā of vast dimensions." *

The two inscriptions are word for word the same, with the exception of the portions dealing with the boundaries of the villages granted. With reference to the foundation of the city, the following points may be noted :

(1) Harihara went out hunting in the forest on the southern bank of the Tungabhadra, where he saw a hound and a hare together, in spite of their natural enmity.

(2) On narrating this incident to Vidyāraṇya who was practising asceticism in the temple of Virūpākṣa, he advised Harihara to found a city on the spot called Vidyānagara.

(3) Harihara accordingly built the city from which he began to rule his kingdom.

* *EC.* x. Bg. 70.

According to these two inscriptions, Harihara I built the city of Vidyānagara on the advice of Vidyāraṇya. However, their evidence cannot be relied upon; for both of them are condemned as spurious; the original of the Yaṟaguḍi grant (Bg. 70) is not available, it "being printed from a hand copy supplied by the people." * The Kāpalūr grant is declared a forgery by the editor:

"The character is Nandināgari but the formation of the letters is quite modern, and in certain letters, it is very similar to Dēvanāgari. This fact shows that the document is a fabrication." †

People who are more competent to pronounce an opinion on the subject have nothing to find fault with the formation of the letters. ‡ Therefore, the genuineness of the inscription cannot be questioned on this ground alone. The strongest objection is based upon the legendary material incorporated in it. No doubt legendary material is found in several inscriptions which are accepted as genuine. But there is a difference. Harihara is said to have witnessed something of an abnormal character, which it is not possible for other human beings to see. That appears to be the most important reason for rejecting the inscription as spurious.

Nevertheless, it is not improbable that Harihara I should have built a capital for himself on the advice of Vidyāraṇya; nor is it unlikely that the city of Vidyānagara or Vijayanagara should have been built about 1336; for, according to some inscriptions, Harihara I was ruling from Vidyānagara in 1348 A.D. §

* *EC.* x. p. 241. n. 1.

† *NDI.* i. p. 109.

‡ Venkayya *IA.* xxxviii. pp. 89-91.

§ *MER.* 1920-21. Part I. A. 9.

But the testimony of the Kāpalūr and the Yaṟaguḍi grants cannot be taken as a proof for the construction of the city by Harihara I in 1336 A. D. Therefore, Harihara's share in the construction of the city must remain doubtful, until some evidence of a more trustworthy character turns up.

Section 2.—Did Vidyāraṇya build a city ? Tradition embodied in works like the Rājakālanirṇaya and Rāyavācaka attribute the construction of Vidyānagara to the sage Vidyāraṇya. But tradition cannot be trusted, and its evidence should not be considered, unless it is corroborated by other reliable sources of information. A few inscriptions of the Tuḷuva period, though they do not attribute the building of the city to Vidyāraṇya, declare that it was built by king Harihara I and named Vidyānagara in the name of Vidyāraṇya Śrīpāda.

It is said in an inscription dated 1538 A. D., that Vidyānagara was built by Harihara Rāya, and was " set up in the name of Vidyāraṇya Śrīpāda." * In another, dated 1559 A.D., Harihara Rāya is said to have built Vidyānagara in the name of Vidyāraṇya." †

Since these inscriptions belong to the 16th century, their evidence should also be classed as traditional. There is, however, one important point which should be noticed. The inscriptions do not make Vidyāraṇya the builder of Vidyānagara. It was Harihara I who built it, and named it after his spiritual advisor Vidyāraṇya. This is not improbable.

Although tradition appears to be untrustworthy, there seems to lurk an element of truth in it. Vidyāraṇya seems to have had some undefined connection with the foundation of the city. The name Vidyānagara

* *EC.* xi Cd. 45. † *ibid.* Cd. 54.

frequently occurs in the inscriptions of the time of Harihara I and Bukka I. It is true that some of them are forgeries, and that the dates of some others are irregular. There are, however, a few which must be taken as genuine. According to A. 16 of 1925-26 Vīrapratāpa Bukkarāya Mahārāya was ruling from Vidyānagara in Ś. 1273 or A.D. 1351. Two inscriptions of Harihara I refer to his capital Vidyānagara. In one inscription dated 1348 A. D., Harihara is said to be ruling from Vidyānagara. * In another dated 1353 A. D., the city is called Kurukṣētra-Vidyānagari. †

If these records are genuine—I believe they are —Vijayanagara had its other name Vidyānagara almost from the very beginning. The same fact is revealed by the literature of the Sangama period. Kallanātha who was a contemporary of Dēvarāya II and Mallikārjuna refers to the capital of his patrons as Vidyānagara. ‡ If the name Vidyānagara was really derived from Vidyāraṇya, as the Tuḷuva inscriptions would have us believe, it cannot be denied that he had some share direct or indirect in building the city.

There is yet another inscription dated 1378 A. D., which attributes the foundation of the city of Vijayanagara to Bukka I.

* A. 9 of 1920-21. † A. 8 of 1925-26.

‡ *JRAS*. 1902 p. 662.

Bhōgasthitā bhōgavatī ca nityam suparvaramyādivijasthalīva
Purīha *Vidyānagarī* cakāsti Tungā tarangai rabhitaḥ pavitrā ||

Ētām śāsti praśasta pratibhaṭa makuṭā prōta niryatna nidrā
Ratna jyōti pravāḷā vanamana caṭulāṭōpa tāpa pratāpaḥ
Karṇāṭāghāṭa Lakṣmī carṇa parilasat pauruṣōtkarṣa śālī
Prauḍha Śrī Dēva Rājō Vijaya Nṛpa sutō Yādavānām varēṇyaḥ ||

Viśvambharā bhāra kṛtāvatāraḥ tasyāsti putrō yaśasā pavitraḥ
Sangīta sāhitya kalāsvabhijñaḥ prātāpavān *Immaḍi Dēvarāyaḥ* ||

Sudharmēva sabhā yasya sam-ullāsi-kalādharā
Gāndharva guṇa gambhīrā vidyādhara vinōdinī. ||

"Having received from him (Harihara I), the wealth of the empire, Bukka rāja, in valour and glory eclipsed all past and future kings. Having conquered all the world, he built a splendid city called the city of Victory." "Its fort walls were like arms stretching out to embrace Hēmakūṭa. The points of its battlements like its filaments, the suburbs like its blossom, the elephants like bees, the hills reflected like stems in the water of the moat, the whole city resembled the lotus on which Lakṣmī is ever seated. There with Tungabhadra as his foot-stool, and Hēmakūṭa as his throne, he (Bukka) was seated like Virūpākṣa, for the protection of the people of the earth." *

The city which, according to the present inscription, Bukka I built cannot be the one whose ruins extend from Hōspēṭ to Ānegondi. It should have been much smaller. The fort was built around the hill of Hēmakūṭa on which the royal palace itself probably stood.

When did Bukka I build this city ? A study of the inscriptions of the time may provide us with the necessary answer, as Vijayanagara is mentioned as the capital of the empire from 1347 A. D., onwards.

Ref.	Date A.D.	Name of the capital.
EC. VIII. Sb. 375 ...	1347	Vijayanagara.
MAR. 1924 Part II. No. 34	1358	do.
E.C XII. Pg. 18 ...	1366	do.
EC. VII. Sk. 281 ...	1368	Abhinava-Vijayanagara.
EC. XII. Mi. 74 ...	1370	Vijayanagara.
MAR. 1914-15 p. 58..	1377	do.

* *EC.* v. Cn. 256.

It is obvious that the city of Vijayanagara was the capital of the kingdom from at least 1347 A. D., *i. e.* almost from the time, when Harihara I, his brothers, and officers met in Śṛngēri to celebrate a festival in commemoration of their conquest of the earth from the Eastern to the Western ocean. Since Harihara I reigned until 1356 A. D., he should have been alive at the time when Bukka I built the capital. No doubt, Bukka I should have been more personally associated with the building of the city than Harihara. Nevertheless, he could not have undertaken the task without the consent and the active co-operation of his elder brother and sovereign. It must, therefore, be admitted that Harihara I should have played some part in the construction of his capital. The truth of the Yaṟaguḍi, and the Kāpalūr grants, so far as the construction of the capital is concerned, is proved indirectly by the inscriptions of the period. It remains to be seen whether Vidyāraṇya Śrīpāda had anything to do with it.

It has become a pastime with a few writers in recent years to treat Vidyāraṇya as a nobody. An unprejudiced investigation of the inscriptions establishes the fact that the early kings of Vijayanagara shaped the course of their conduct on his advice. Vidyāraṇya is mentioned in several inscriptions of Bukka I and Harihara II. He was the spiritual advisor of the latter. "By the grace of Vidyāraṇya *muni*, he acquired the empire of knowledge unattainable by other kings." * The influence of the *gurus* over their disciples is well-known. It is not unreasonable to think that Harihara II would have consulted him on important mattters of policy. The relations between Bukka I and Vidyāraṇya appear to have been more

* *MAR.* 1916, p. 56.

intimate. He was in the habit of accompanying the sage when the latter visited Śṛṅgēri to meet his *guru.* * He seems to have felt, at least on occasions, that the presence of Vidyāraṇya at Vijayanagara was indispensable. About 1356 A. D., Vidyāraṇya paid a visit to Benares where he stayed for sometime. Bukka I, who must have succeeded Harihara I during that year, desired for some reason that Vidyāraṇya should return to Vijayanagara. He knew that his request to the sage would not induce the latter to leave Benares. He therefore obtained a *śrīmukha* from the Senior Śrīpāda of Śṛṅgēri, commanding Vidyāraṇya to return to Vidyānagara, and despatched it to him coupled with his own request. It is said that he obeyed the order gladly, "as he had great respect for his *guru.*" † Two points should be noticed here. (1) Bukka felt for some reason that the presence at Vijayanagara of Vidyāraṇya was necessary. (2) To secure this end, he was convinced that he should obtain the help of the Senior Śrīpāda of Śṛṅgēri.

What made Bukka think that Vidyāraṇya would not return to Vijayanagara at his own request? Because he knew that the sage who retired to Benares to spend his time in contemplation would not return to Vijayanagara, as it would involve him once again in the affairs of the world. Vidyāraṇya as Mādhavācārya before he became a *sanyāsin* was a minister of Bukka. It is said in the Parāśara Mādhavīya that Mādhavācārya was the *kulaguru* as well as the minister of Bukka. "Like Āngirasa to Indra, Sumati to Nala, Medhātithi to Śaibya, Dhanuja to Rāma, Mādhava was the *kulaguru* as well as the minister to king Bukka." ‡ Probably Bukka wanted Vidyāraṇya

* *MAR.* 1916, p. 56. † *ibid.*

‡ Parāśara Mādhavīya : Introduction to the Vyavahāra Kāṇḍa.

at Vijayanagara, so that he might have the benefit of the counsel of the sage as of old. It is customary even at the present day among the Hindus to consult men of learning and piety when they desire to build a house, for the purpose of discovering the most auspicious time for commencing operations. Would not Harihara I and Bukka I have consulted somebody when they resolved to build a new capital? Who was there more competent to advise them on such a matter than Vidyāraṇya? Harihara II, and probably also Bukka I held him in high estimation. His feats are said to be 'more wonderful than those of Brahma,' for he could 'make the most eloquent dumb and the dumb, most eloquent.' * The following passage culled from an inscription of Harihara II describes how great Vidyāraṇya looked in the eyes of his contemporaries :—

"May the wonderful glances of Vidyāraṇya which resemble showers of camphor dust, garlands of *kalhāra* flower, rays of the moon, sandal paste, and waves of milk ocean, and which shower the nectar of compassion, bring you happiness. Can he be Brahma? We do not see four faces. Can he be Viṣṇu? He has not got four arms. Can he be Śiva? No oddness of the eye is observed. Having thus argued for a long time, the learned have come to the conclusion that Vidyāraṇya is the supreme light incarnate." †

Would not Harihara I and Bukka I have consulted this 'supreme light incarnate?' It is not unlikely that they sought his advice, and began to construct the city after he blessed their enterprise. When the construction of the city was completed they gave it the name of Vidyānagara in honour of the *guru* whom they adored. This conclusion is corroborated, as we had already noticed, by inscriptions containing references to Vidyānagara as early as 1348 A.D.

* *MAR*. 1916 p. 56. † *ibid*.

PART II

THE ORIGIN OF THE EMPIRE

CHAPTER I

BALLĀḶA III AND THE SONS OF SANGAMA

Section 1 :—The circumstances under which the kingdom of Vijayanagara was founded still remain in obscurity, in spite of the efforts of several scholars during the last three decades. It has been said that the five brothers who founded the kingdom of Vijayanagara, were originally in the service of the Hoysala king Vīra Ballāḷa III, who employed them to defend his northern frontier and "to stem the new flood of the Bahmani invasions." * The places which were entrusted to the care of the five brothers are also described. "In the early wars of Alā-ud-Din Bahmani, when he marched south from Daulatābad after the death of Muhammad bin Tughlak, there figures on the southern frontier, and therefore the more uncertain frontier of his, a Hindu chieftain of the name of Harib in the region of the Konkan coast up to Jamkhaṇḍi. A little further to the east of it between Bijāpūr and Gulburga figures another Hindu chief by name Kaprās ; and further east another Hindu chieftain still of the name of Kamprāz. . . . These three Hindu chieftains are obviously no other than Hariappa (Harib), Bukkappa Rāzu (Kaprās), and Kampa Rāzu (Kampaṇa, Kamprāz), the three elder of the five brothers to whom the inscriptions of the time ascribe the foundation of the empire of Vijayanagara." † The tract of territory over which Kampa Rāzu bore sway has also been definitely described. "The government of the Nellore district, with the fortified hill of Udayagiri within its jurisdiction, was a

* South India and her Muhammadan Invaders p. 181.

† *ibid*.

very important post as regards strategy in Southern India. . . . The importance of the post was specially relevant when the Mussalmans of Delhi had shortly before captured the city of Warangal, the capital of the Kākatīya Dynasty just to the north of Udayagiri." "Kampa was therefore placed in that responsible post by the same Vīra Ballāḷa (III)." *

Opinion, however, is divided regarding the manner in which the independent kingdom of Vijayanagara came into being. Some hold that after the death of Ballāḷa III, the five brothers having asserted their independence established a new state with the city of Vijayanagara as its capital; † whereas others believe that Ballāḷa 'countenanced Harihara's (the eldest of the five brothers) establishing himself further north as a great lord, and supported him by allowing him to rule locally in the very heart of the Hoysala kingdom.' ‡ It is even asserted that 'Harihara I was enthroned at Vijayanagara by the old Hoysala monarch (Ballāḷa III) as his own Mahāmaṇḍalēśvara in the north.' §

It follows from this that,

(1) the five brothers who established the kingdom of Vijayanagara were the subordinates of Vīra Ballāḷa III.

(2) the Hoysala dominions, the defence of which was entrusted to the care of the five brothers extended

* Heras: *The Beginnings* pp. 94-95 Cf. S. K. Iyengar. *HAI.* p. 35. 'Another important garrison was placed (by Ballāḷa III) at Udayagiri in the Nellore district to guard the eastern highway.'

† Kṛṣṇa Śāstri: *ASR.* 1907-8. p. 236.

‡ Sewell: *Historical Inscriptions*, p. 187.

§ Heras: *The Beginnings*, p. 67.

from the Arabian Sea in the west to the Bay of Bengal in the east, including along its northern frontier the territory corresponding to the modern districts of North Canara, Dhārwār, Bijāpūr and Nellore.

(3) the Hoysala kingdom was exposed to the attacks of the Bahmani Sultan Alā-ud-Din I, whom the five brothers were expected to check.

(4) Ballāḷa III enthroned Harihara I at Vijayanagara, probably to induce him to take a personal interest in the protection of the realm.

Unless these propositions are closely examined, it is not possible to discover how far they are true.

Section 2 :—(1) No evidence in support of this proposition is forthcoming. Nearly three hundred and fifty inscriptions of Ballāḷa III have been brought to light so far. It is strange that, if the five brothers who founded the kingdom of Vijayanagara were really Ballāḷa's subordinates, they should not have been mentioned in any of them. It is believed that a certain prince called Kaṭhōra-Hara is mentioned in a Citaldrug inscription dated A. D. 1328. * An attempt has been made to identify this Kaṭhōra-Hara with 'Harihara I of Vijayanagara who in all probability was one of those kinsmen summoned to the meeting of Tiruvaṇṇāmalai.' † It is pointed out that 'on many occasions Harihara's name is cut short and only the first part is given, thus Hariyappa. Perhaps on this occasion the first part is omitted so that the epithet Kaṭhōra (fierce) should be properly applied to Hara or Śiva. In fact Kaṭhōra is the thirty-seventh name of Śiva. This

* *EC.* xi. Cd. 4.

† Heras: *The Beginnings*, p. 125.

would be a welcome piece of flattery for Harihara.' * The explanation is no doubt ingenious, but it is uncalled for; for the name Kaṭhōra-Hara does not at all occur in the text of the inscription. † It is, therefore, evident that among the officers and dependents of Ballāḷa III, there was no person bearing the name of Kaṭhōra-Hara. Consequently the question of his identification does not arise. Again the numerous inscriptions of Harihara I and his brothers do not even allude to their connection with Ballāḷa III. On the contrary, they make it clear that the founders of Vijayanagara were independent rulers from the very beginning. In the absence of evidence of any kind, it is not reasonable to suppose that Harihara I and his brothers were at first subordinates of Vīra Ballāḷa III.

Section 3 :—(2) What was the extent of the Hoysala dominions during the reign of Ballāḷa III? The kingdom which he came to rule after the demise of his father Narasimha III in 1292 A. D., was very limited in extent. It corresponded roughly to the present Mysore state excluding Kōlār, and portions of Bangalore, Tumkūr, Citaldrug and Ṣīmoga districts. Even this small kingdom, he was not suffered to rule in peace. He had to face the attacks of his uncle Rāmanātha, who wanted to deprive him of his kingdom, and throne. Rāmanātha was a half-brother of Narasimha III; and their father Sōmēśwara divided his kingdom equally between his two sons, giving the Tamil districts to the former, and the Canarese districts which formed the Hoysala kingdom properly so called to the latter. The reign of Sōmēśwara, however, ended in a disaster. He was killed about 1262 A. D., in a battle with Jaṭāvarman Sundara Pāṇḍyadēva

* Heras : *The Beginnings*, p. 125. n. 1.

‡ Supra pp. 9-10.

(A. D. 1250-1273) *, the king of Madura, and his capital Kannanūr was captured. † It was probably at this time that Vīra-Pāṇḍya invaded Kongu which he annexed to the Paṇḍyan dominions. ‡ Rāmanātha was thus threatened with the loss of his patrimony; but he seems to have managed somehow to recapture Kannanūr from which he ruled his territory in the Cōḷa country until 1280 A. D., when he was finally driven out of it by the Pāṇḍyas. Having thus lost most of what his father had given him, he wanted to compensate for his loss at the expense of his half-brother. This led to the outbreak of a war between the two brothers which dragged on for nearly thirty years.

The struggle seems to have commenced even before Rāmanātha's final expulsion from the Cōḷa country. It is alluded to in an undated inscription of the Hāssan district which Rice assigns to about 1260 A. D. § This date is too early for the outbreak of the war. In the first place, Sōmēśwara was still alive, and it is extremely unlikely that he would have allowed his two sons to quarrel with each other over the division of the kingdom which he himself had

* Sōmēśwara is said to have died in A. D. 1257 (*EC.* iv. Kr. 9). This is improbable, as we find several of his inscriptions dated in his 27th and 29th regnal years corresponding to 1259 and 1261 respectively. (*MER.* 20 of 1891, 519 of 1912, 34 of 1891.)

† *EI.* iii. p. 14.

‡ Kongu remained under the Pāṇḍyas probably until 1320 A. D. Several inscriptions of Vīra-Pāṇḍya refer to his conquest of Kongu (*e. g.* 35 of 1923); and the existence of a few of his inscriptions in the Coimbatore district prove the truth of the assertion. An epigraph from Sērmādēvi attributes the conquest of the two Kongus to Māravarman Kulaśēkhara. Although Kulaśēkhara's records are not found in the Kongu country, we find some of his co-regent Jaṭāvarman Sundara Pāṇḍya in that region. The Pāṇḍyan occupation of Kongu is confirmed by the total absence of the Hoysala inscriptions. No inscription of Narasimha III nor of Rāmanātha is found in the Coimbatore district; and the earliest dated inscription of Ballāḷa III belongs to the year 1323 A. D. (588 of 1904).

§ *EC.* v. Cn. 206.

effected. Secondly, the Hoysala position in the South was challenged by the Pāṇḍyas at this time, and Rāmanātha could not have found it safe to despatch an army against his brother.

However, there is reason to believe that his first attack was delivered sometime before A. D. 1270; for an inscription dated in that year coming from the Cannarāyapaṭṭaṇa tālūka of the Hāssan district mentions Rāmanātha as the reigning sovereign. * As he is said to have been still ruling from Kannanūr, he could not have concentrated all his attention upon the conquest of Narasimha's dominions. A more serious expedition seems to have been undertaken in A. D. 1278, when he is said to have raised the villages of Mannaṇakōgil and fought and killed a certain Singeya Daṇṇāyaka who was probably one of Narasimha's officers. † On this occasion Rāmanātha seems to have united his forces with those of '. . . arasa Gajapati,' and offered battle to his brother at Sōlelūr. ‡ It was probably in this battle that Lāla Māceya, one of Narasimha's subordinates was killed. § An epigraph dated 1282 A. D. records the death of another officer of Narasimha called Koṇḍu Nāyaka in a battle with Rāmanātha. ¶ Whether Koṇḍu Nāyaka's death is connected with this war or some other cannot be ascertained at present. The war seems to have ended in a compromise, the terms of which, however, are not recorded. In the meanwhile Rāmanātha seems to have lost his hold on the Cōḷa country completely. None of his inscriptions belonging to a date subsequent to his 25th year corresponding to 1279 A. D., is

* *EC.* v. Cn. 231.

† *ibid.* Ak. 149.

‡ *ibid.* Bl. 187.

§ *MAR.* 1909, p. 22.

¶ *EC.* v. Hn. 47.

found in the south. He was still ruling from his capital Kannanūr in 1278; * but he was soon driven out of it by the great Pāṇḍyan monarch Māravarman Kulaśēkhara. It is stated in an inscription dated in Kulaśēkhara's 15th year (1283) that he was 'in his camp at Kannanūr.' † Consequently Rāmanātha was obliged to abandon the Cōḷa country, and shift his capital to Hesar-Kundāṇi in the Salem district from which he was ruling what was left of his old kingdom in 1287. ‡

The loss of most of his kingdom, coupled with a desire to provide for his son, probably induced Rāmanātha to violate the terms of the compromise with Narasimha III, and embark once again on a policy of aggressive conquest. He seems to have devoted the last seven years of his life in waging war with his brother and nephew. The campaign opened with the siege of the fort of Beṭṭadakōṭe in the Guṇḍlupēṭa tālūka of the Mysore district where there appears to have been some severe fighting. § Probably the place was taken, and Rāmanātha next seems to have marched upon his brother's capital, Dōrasamudra. A battle was fought in which some of the officers of Narasimha III were killed. ¶ Since Ballāḷa III was residing in 1291 in Dōrasamudra, ‖ where he was anointed in the next year, ** it is reasonable to believe that Rāmanātha's attempt to capture Dōrasamudra was not successful. Nevertheless, he seems to have annexed a good slice of Narasimha's territory in the east, comprising the

* *EC.* v. Ak. 149.

† *MER.* 328 of 1923; Nīlakaṇṭha Śāstri: *The Pāṇḍyas* p. 184 n. 1.

‡ *EC.* xiii. Tm. 17, 27, 28, 29, 33.

§ *MAR.* 1916, p. 55.

¶ *EC.* v. Cn. 232.

‖ *Ibid.* vi. Kd. 49.

** *Ibid.* Cm. 36.

eastern tālūkas of the present Bangalore and Tumkūr districts. While the war was still going on, Narasimha III died, * and he was succeeded by his son Vīra Ballāḷa III who was anointed, as already noticed, in 1292. Ballāḷa thus found himself in the midst of a war at the very beginning of his reign. Rāmanātha seems to have turned his attention to Sīgal nāḍu which he overran during the same year. † In the next year he laid siege to the fortress of Kuṇigal, where he seems to have met with stubborn resistance. The defenders fought with the besiegers 'like wrestlers,' though the town was ultimakely taken. Some of them are said to have penetrated into the ranks of the enemy, and perished on their swords as they were unwilling to be taken prisoners. ‡ The capture of Kuṇigal appears to be the last episode of the war. No information is available regarding the events which happened subsequent to the fall of this fort. The illness from which Rāmanātha seems to have been suffering during the last three years of his reign § may possibly have resulted in the cessation of hostilities and the conclusion of peace. Rāmanātha breathed his last in 1295, ¶ and was succeeded by his son Viśwanātha who ruled for a short period of three or four years, though nothing is known about the events that happened in his reign. With his death, the Tamil branch of the Hoysala family became extinct, and consequently the Hoysala dominions were re-united under Ballāḷa III.

The death of Viśwanātha freed Ballāḷa III from an enemy who might become dangerous at any time ; and the expansion of his dominions caused by the addition

* *EC.* iv. Kr. 10; *MAR.* 1915, p. 56. † *ibid* ix. Kn. 28.

‡ *ibid* ix. Cp. 183. § *Ibid*. x. Bp. 23, 25 a ; Ct. 88.

¶ The date of his death is nowhere recorded. As Bp. 25 a dated in 1295 is his last records, it may be inferred that he died in that year.

of his cousin's territory increased his resources, and strengthened his position. He was now ready to turn his attention to external conquest. He seems to have come into conflict with the Pāṇḍyas about 1297, for, he is styled 'the conqueror of the Pāṇḍya' in an epigraph of Heḍatale in the Nañjangūḍ tālūka. * The Pāṇḍya whom he conquered about this time should have been one of the numerous Āḷupa chiefs that were ruling on the west coast; but his attention should have been drawn to the north rather than the west; for, the extensive Yādava dominions lay almost unprotected owing to the invasion of Alā-ud-Din Khilji. Some of the Sēuṇa feudataries had thrown off the yoke of Dēvagiri, and were busy in carving out kingdoms for themselves. The time, therefore, should have appeared very opportune for launching an attack on the territories belonging to the Sēuṇas who were the hereditary enemies of Ballāḷa's family.

The feud between the Hoysalas and the Sēuṇas was rooted in the past. It had its origin during the last quarter of the twelfth century when the country was seething with confusion and political unrest. In 1176, Sankama Dēva of the Kālacurya dynasty ascended the throne which his father had usurped from the Cāḷukyas; † but from the day of his accession he had to face several troubles. Sōmēśwara IV, the last of the Cāḷukyas was striving hard to regain the kingdom which his father had lost. About A. D. 1182, his general Brahma, wrested from the Kālacuryas a large part of the kingdom. ‡ The supremacy had thus passed once again from the Kālacuryas to the Cāḷukyas. As Sōmēśwara IV was not a strong ruler,

* *EC.* iv. Nj. 95; *MAR.* 1918. p. 47.

† Fleet, *Dyn. Kan. Dts.* pp. 486-87. ‡ *Ibid* p. 464.

many feudatories of his family taking advantage of his incapacity asserted their independence. The Sēuṇas appropriated the northern districts; the Hoysalas established themselves in the south; and the Kākatīyas made themselves masters of the east. In addition to these, there arose througout the kingdom, several petty principalities which showed no inclination to submit to anyone. Moreover, the ambitious policies pursued by the rulers of the three kingdoms, brought them often into conflict with one another which resulted in the outbreak of bloody and protracted wars.

Sōmēśwara had to maintain his authority over these turbulent feudatories. Although he succeeded in exercising some power for a few years, he had at last to succumb to the inevitable. His general, Brahma was defeated by the Hoysala Vīra Ballāḷa II *, and whatever power he might have exercised before this, completely vanished with the disaster. The disappearance of Sōmēśwara IV from the political arena left his nominal feudatories free to grab as much of his territory as they could seize. The land-hunger naturally engendered war and very soon the peaceful countryside became disturbed by the marches of the contending armies †. The bone of contention was the doab between the Kṛṣṇa and the Tungabhadra. At the commencement of the period, a large portion of this area passed into the hands of the Sēuṇa chief, Bhillama, who consequently assumed the title of "the beloved of the goddess of the sovereignty of Karṇāṭa country." ‡ His sway, however, did not extend over the whole of Karṇāṭa, as the Hoysalas of Dōrasamudra, the Pāṇḍyas of Ucchangi, and the Kadambas

* Fleet: *Dyn. Kan. Dts.* p. 502.

† *MER.* F. 113 of 1926-27.

‡ Fleet: *Dyn. Kan. Dts.* p. 518.

of Goa and Hānangal among others did not acknowledge his supremacy. He was not even allowed to rule peacefully that bit of Karṇāṭa which he had won ; for his right to rule Karṇāṭa was soon questioned, and he was ousted from his place by a successful rival, Vīra Ballāḷa II, the king of the Hoysalas.

Ballāḷa II ascended the throne in A. D. 1173 *. During the first ten years of his reign he was busy consolidating his position by effecting the conquest of some petty principalities in his neighbourhood. The Cengāḷvas were conquered in 1173 ; † and the Pāṇḍyan fort of Ucchangi in the Nōlambavāḍi was subjugated in 1177. ‡ About 1179, he fought with the Kālacurya king, Sankama Dēva whom he defeated. § It was probably during these years that he acquired the tract of country corresponding to the western half of the present Beḷḷāry district. Having thus strengthened his position, he commenced the struggle with the Cāḷukyas and the Sēuṇas for establishing his supremacy over Northern Karṇāṭa. His victory over Brahma, the general of Sōmēśwara, has already been noticed. He penetrated into the Dhārwār country, and attacked Bhillama. A decisive battle was fought at Soraṭūr in the Gaḍag tālūka in A. D. 1191-2, and Ballāḷa won a glorious victory. ¶ It was probably on this occasion that he slew Jaitrasimha, the trusted minister and general of Bhillama. Most of Northern Karṇāṭa consequently passed into the hands of the Hoysala king. The extent of his territory excluding the Gangavāḍi, Ninety-six Thousand country is described in an inscription of Hirehaḍagalli. It embraced Nōlambavāḍi 32000,

* *EC.* v. Hn. 119 ; Hn. 71 vi Rd. 4, 136, 129.

† *ibid* Bl. 86.

‡ *EC.* iv. Ng. 70.

§ *MAR.* 1915 Para 81.

¶ *IA.* ii. p. 299.

Banavāse 12000, Huḷigere 300, the two Beḷuvoḷas, and Masavāḍi right up to Heddore. * A portion of Sindavādi 1000 seems to have been included in it; for Ballāḷa II's inscriptions are found as far north-east as Kurugōḍu in the Beḷḷāry district. † Although Ballāḷa II's authority extended over portions of North Canara, Dhārwār, Rāicūr, and Beḷḷāry districts, it was never recognised on the northern banks of the Kṛṣṇa and the Mālaprabha. The northern boundary of the "Hoysala kingdom," it is said, "was evidently the Mālaprabha river, and the Kṛṣṇa from the point where the Mālaprabha joins it." ‡ All the inscriptions of Ballāḷa II are found only to the south of these rivers, none being found on the north.

Ballāḷa II ruled the conquered country undisturbed for nearly twenty years. His authority was then challenged by the Sēuṇa king, Singhaṇa, a grandson of his old enemy, Bhillama. Though it is generally believed that Singhaṇa ascended the throne in A. D. 1210, available epigraphic evidence seems to indicate that the event should have taken place, at least seven years earlier. An inscription of Dēvarabeṭṭa in the Ādōni tālūka dated in A. D. 1210 is said to correspond to his 6th regnal year. § Another inscription from Peddakottalika in the same tālūka is dated in A. D. 1203; ¶ a third epigraph from Gōranṭla in the Kurnool tālūka is dated in A. D. 1205. ‖ It is obvious that Singhaṇa was governing the kingdom from A. D. 1203 to 1210, though his activities during this period are yet unknown. His struggle with Ballāḷa II did not commence until 1210. It is stated in an

* *MER.* 495 of 1914.

† *ibid* 68 of 1904.

‡ Fleet: *Dyn. Kan. Dts.* p. 519.

§ *MER.* 498 of 1915.

¶ *ibid.* 552 of 1915.

‖ *VR.* i. Kl. 221.

inscription dated in the cyclic year Vyaya corresponding to A. D. 1226 that it was sixteen years since Singhaṇa entered the Dhārwār country *. Therefore, the Sēuṇa reconquest of Dhārwār should have begun in A. D. 1210. Ballāḷa II seems to have held his own for at least two years; for the latest date of his inscriptions in Dhārwār is 1212, † after which no Hoysala record is found in any part of the district. He was then forced to retire into his own country which became the objective of a series of Sēuṇa invasions during the succeeding years. Two inscriptions from the Sorab tālūka dated respectively in 1211 and 1212 allude to an invasion of Singhaṇadēva. ‡ Another undated epigraph from Mallāpura refers to an expedition which Ballāḷa II had despatched under the command of Mahādēva Daṇṇāyaka against Singhaṇadēva. § These records indicate that there was severe fighting in the north-western Mysore between the Hoysalas and the Sēuṇas in which the latter seems to have gained the upperhand. A study of the inscriptions reveals the fact that the Sēuṇas displaced the Hoysalas in parts of the Ṣīmoga and Citaldrug districts either during the reign of Ballāḷa II or in that of his successor. ¶ The Hoysala power was put an end to in the Sorab tālūka in 1212; and although Sōmēśwara seems to have made a few sporadic efforts to regain what was lost by his grandfather, the Sēuṇas managed to maintain their rule probably until 1310. A. D. Though the last Sēuṇa inscription is dated in 1300, the earliest of Ballāḷa III is assigned to 1314. It is not unlikely that Rāmacandra, in spite of his several misfortunes, was able to

* *MER.* E. 27 of 1927-28. † *ibid.* F. 52 of 1926-27.

‡ *EC.* viii, Sb. 376 Sb. 404. § *MAR.* 1927, No. 156.

¶ See Appendix A for this as well as the discussion regarding the relations between the Sēuṇas and the Hoysalas.

keep a semblance of his authority until his death. The Hoysala rule lasted in Sāgar until 1226. Singhaṇa seems to have conquered it during the reign of Narasimha II or that of his son. It was not until 1299 that the Hoysalas could secure a footing in the region once again. In Ṣikārpūr, the rule of Ballāḷa II was brought to an end in A. D. 1215, and the Sēuṇas held undisputed sway over the tālūka until 1294-5. Honnaḷi tālūka passed into the hands of the Sēuṇas in 1215; and in spite of the attacks of Narasimha III, it remained in their possession until 1294. Since the earliest of Ballāḷa III's inscriptions is assigned to A. D. 1314, the Sēuṇa rule may be supposed to have continued until the end. The exact date of the conquest of the Cannagiri tālūka cannot be ascertained. The last Hoysala inscription is dated in 1233, the last year of the reign of Narasimha II. Neither Sōmēśwara, nor Narasimha III is represented even by a single record. It is obvious that the Hoysalas had lost their hold on the region subsequent to the death of Narasimha II; but the earliest Sēuṇa grant belongs to 1265. It is not known when between 1233 and 1265 this area passed from the Hoysalas to the Sēuṇas. Dāvaṇagere was the only tālūka of the Citaldrug district, conquered by the Sēuṇas. The conquest seems to have been effected during the last days of Singhaṇa. Notwithstanding the feeble attempts of Narasimha III to dislodge the Sēuṇas, they remained in this part of the country till at least 1303. The Hoysala authority in the Beḷḷāry district came to an end, as already noticed, during the reign of Sōmēśwara. Rāmanātha, no doubt, led an expedition as far as Kōgḷi in 1275-6, * but his rule did not take root in the soil. It may be said that the Sēuṇas not only succeeded in driving the Hoysalas out

* *MER.* 33, 34 of 1904.

of North Karṇāṭa but established themselves permanently in a strip of Hoysala territory to the south of the Tungabhadra extending from Beḷḷāry in the east to the Western Ghats. The territory lost by the Hoysalas between 1212 and 1292 roughly corresponded in extent to Banavāse, Nōlambavāḍi, the Beḷvoḷas, Masavāḍi, and Sindavāḍi.

Ballāḷa III set his mind on the recovery of the territory lost by his predecessors. His war with the Sēuṇas seems to have begun in 1299. He made an attack upon Kōṭi Nāyaka, the ruler of Santalige Thousand, and laid siege to his capital Hosaguṇḍa which he captured *. He took Kōṭi Nāyaka prisoner, and carried off his elephant. † Erupeya Daṇṇāyaka, one of his own officers, was appointed the ruler of the district. ‡ It has been suggested that Kōṭi Nāyaka was one of the refractory chiefs, who rose up in revolt against Ballāḷa III; § but Santalige Thousand was conquered by the Sēuṇa general Paraśurāmadēva in 1293; ¶ and therefore, at the time of Ballāḷa's invasion it should have been a Sēuṇa dependency, or what is more likely an independent principality having thrown off the Sēuṇa yoke subsequent to Alā-ud-Din's attack upon Dēvagiri in 1295. Be that as it may. Ballāḷa III's appetite for conquest became keener by his initial success; he invaded the province of Banavāse in 1300, and lay encamped in the neighbourhood of the village of Sirisi. ‖ The presence of Ballāḷa in their country seem to have united all the chiefs of the district under the leadership of Gangeya Sāhiṇi, the great minister of

* *EC.* viii. Sa. 96, 98.

† *ibid.* Sa. 45.

‡ *ibid.* Sa. 62.

§ *The Mysore Gazetteer*: (New Edition). Vol. II Part ii p. 1399.

¶ *EC.* viii. Sa. 102.

‖ *ibid.* Sa. 45.

the Kadamba prince, Kāvadēva. In the battle that was fought on the occasion, Ballāḷa III was defeated and driven back. This reverse, however, did not deter him from his purpose, and he repeated his attack on Banavāse three years later, and pitched his tents once again at Sirisi where he was formerly defeated.* Gangeya Sāhiṇi having mustered his troops offered him battle but the result of the engagement is not known. The progress of the invasion should have been greatly checked owing to a diversion caused by the Sēuṇa attack on the north-eastern frontier of the Hoysala dominions. At the command of king Rāmadēva, his general Kampiladēva advanced upon Holāḷkere and took it.† He then entered the principality of Bemmaṭanakallu, and inflicted a defeat upon its ruler, Sōmeya Nāyaka.‡ This seems to have produced the desired effect; and Ballāḷa III was obliged to keep his plans of conquest in abeyance at least for one year. However, he invaded the Sēuṇa kingdom in 1304, and laid siege to Nakkiguṇḍi, which he captured after winning a victory over the enemy.§ Rāmadēva, who seems to have been greatly angered by the persistent attacks upon his kingdom, took personally the command of the army in order to push back the invader. Both the armies met somewhere in the Banavāse country and a sanguinary battle took place. While issuing the order for battle, Rāmadēva commanded his officers saying "you must take the king of Karṇāṭakas, and seize and give me that tiger's cub." On this, his soldiers rushed upon the enemy, and 'making no hesitation' 'performed various exploits.' It is not known how the battle ended. Probably Ballāḷa III was able to keep his hold on what he had

* *EC.* viii. Sa. 101.

† *MAR.* 1913, p. 50.

‡ *MAR.* 1913, p. 45.

§ *EC.* ix. Bn. 53.

grasped. With this battle the struggle between the Sēuṇas and the Hoysalas may be said to have come to an end, for no encounter is recorded during the subsequent years.

Ballāḷa devoted his attention during the next two years to the reduction of the fort of Niḍugal in the Anantapūr district. Niḍugal was the capital of a small but powerful Cōḷa principality the rulers of which had been hostile to the Hoysalas since the middle of the thirteenth century. Irungoḷadēva II, accompanied by his friend Gūḷeya Nāyaka, led an attack upon the fort of Ānebidderisi in the Tumkūr tālūka in 1269. * He also participated in the attack of the Sēuṇa general, Sāḷuva Tikkama on Dōrasamudra in 1276. † It was only natural that Hoysala Narasimha III should have retaliated. He marched upon the fort in 1285, and after a siege of a few months captured it; ‡ but it was retaken by Baica *Camūpati*, the minister of Gaṇēśwaradēva, a grandson of Irungoḷa II, § and it remained in the possession of the Cōḷas ever since. The reduction of Niḍugal is not mentioned in any of Ballāḷa III's records. He was fighting with somebody in 1307, for a grant was made during that year for the victory of his sword and arm. ¶ He is mentioned for the first time as the ruler of Niḍugal in an inscription dated A. D. 1308. ‖ It is reasonable to suppose that the conquest had taken place before that date. As he was busy from 1292 to 1305 fighting either with his uncle, Rāmanātha or with the Sēuṇas, it is unlikely that he could have found time to undertake this conquest during those years. Therefore, the subjugation of

* *EC.* xii. Tm. 49.

† *ibid*, v. Bl. 164, 165.

‡ *ibid*. Ak. 151 ; *MAR*. 1909 p. 22.

§ *EC.* xii. Pg. 53.

¶ *MAR*. 1914 (*EC*. x. *MR*. 83 revised.)

‖ *MER*. 729 of 1917.

Niḍugal should have taken place either in 1306 or in the succeeding year. Ballāḷa appointed Aḷiya Māceya Daṇṇāyaka as the governor of the conquered territory; but the people did not remain docile; and on occasions they caused much trouble to Aḷiya Māceya and his sons. * In spite of the disturbances which broke the peace now and then, the Hoysala power was never seriously impaired and the district remained in the possession of Aḷiya Māceya's family until 1340. †

The Hoysala connection with the south ceased, as noticed already, about 1280 A. D., when Rāmanātha had to abandon Cōḷa *maṇḍala,* and retire to a new capital at Hesar-Kundāṇi. The country which for two generations the Hoysalas ruled was occupied by the Pāṇḍyan monarch, Māravarman Kulaśēkhara. The Pāṇḍyan rule remained undisturbed for nearly thirty years; but towards the close of the first decade of the fourteenth century, a civil war broke out in the Pāṇḍyan kingdom owing to the rivalry between Vīra Pāṇḍya and Sundara Pāṇḍya, the two sons of Kulaśēkhara. This was an opportunity which Ballāḷa III could not allow to pass unnoticed. Therefore, he marched on the territory of the Pāṇḍyan brothers "for the purpose of sacking their two empty cities and plundering the merchants." ‡ He was, however, balked of his prey by the intrusion of an enemy of whose advance he seems to have been totally unaware.

Alā-ud-Din Khilji who ascended the throne of Delhi in 1296, had despatched an expedition under the command of Malik Kāfūr against the Hindu kingdoms of Deccan and South India in 1310. The expedition reached Dēvagiri, and was welcomed by Rāmadēva who

* *MAR.* 772 of 1917. † *ibid.* 102 of 1926-27.

‡ *ED.* iii. p. 88

remained loyal to his sovereign since 1295. He provided the Mussalman army with the necessary supplies, and commanded his *daḷavāy,* Paraśurāmadēva to act as its guide on the march to Dōrasamudra, the capital of Ballāḷa III. * On hearing of the advance of the Muhammadan army, Ballāḷa was obliged to return to his country for the purpose of organising its defence. The Muhammadan historians make it appear that he surrendered without any resistance. The truth seems to be quite the opposite. It is said in two inscriptions assigned to 1310, that one of Ballāḷa's officers called Baica Nāyaka perished in a battle with the Muhammadans. † And an epigraph dated 1316 refers to the rebuilding of his residence at Dōrasamudra. ‡ It is evident from these, that Ballāḷa fought at least one or two battles with the Mussalmans before he allowed them to approach his capital, which they ultimately besieged and partly destroyed. Having realised the futility of further resistance, he sued for and obtained peace by surrendering all his wealth.

The Muhammadan invasion exhausted Ballāḷa's resources and paralysed his strength. He remained thoroughly inactive during the next few years engaging himself in repairing the damage done to his capital and kingdom by the invaders. He appears to have been so far successful in recovering his strength, that in 1317 he launched forth an expedition of conquest against Tulu nāḍ. An army under the command of Sankiya Sāhiṇi, a brother-in-law of Ballāḷa III's senior house minister, Bāceya Daṇṇāyaka marched against Basavadēva of Candāvūr below the ghats. § He demolished the town, and proceeded

* *ED.* iii. pp. 87-88.

† *EC.* v. Hn. 51, 52.

‡ *EC.* iv. Md. 100.

§ *EC.* vii. Hl. 117.

against a place called Mutt. . . . . , where a battle was fought in which the Tuḷuva army is said to have been destroyed. The small principality of Sētu was probably subdued at this time, as the chief of the place had become a subordinate of Ballāḷa III sometime before 1320. * The conquest of Tulu nāḍ extending as far as Bārakūr and Mangalore was completed sometime before 1333 A. D. As a mark of his victory over the Āḷupas, Ballāḷa seems to have assumed the Āḷupa title, Pāṇḍya Cakravartin. †

While the campaign in Tulu nāḍ was still in progress, Ballāḷa III had to intervene in the affairs of the Pāṇḍyan kingdom. The Muhammadan invasion seems to have scarcely affected the course of the civil war. Vīra Pāṇḍya, the eldest son of Kulaśēkhara was governing the northern districts of the kingdom from his capital Kannanūr. He was attacked by his son Samudra Pāṇḍya whom Parākrama Pāṇḍya, another chief of the family had joined. Vīra Pāṇḍya whose position was not probably strong seems to have invited Ballāḷa III to go to his assistance, and the latter appears to have readily accepted the invitation. ‡ Ballāḷa marched at the head of an army and reached in 1318 Aruṇasamudra § which he made his headquarters for the time being. He is said to have been marching in 1318 from Kannanūr to some unknown destination, when he was attacked by the enemy. ¶ The result of the action is not recorded, but it is not unlikely that he sustained a defeat. The progress of his campaign was checked suddenly by the appearance of the Muhammadans on his northern frontier. Mubārak

* *EC.* viii. Nr. 19.

† *MER.* 1928-29, ii. p. 81.

‡ *MAR.* 1913, p. 41.

§ *EC.* ix. Cp. 73; *MAR.* 1916 p. 55.

¶ *EC.* xii. Ck. 4.

Shāh Khilji who ascended the throne of Delhi in A. D. 1317, marched personally at the head of his army to subdue Harapāladēva of Dēvagiri who rose up in revolt. He captured Harapāla, and flayed him alive. On this occasion, the Sultān remained at Dēvagiri for some months when he subjugated the whole of Mahārāṣṭra and divided it among his officers. At the same time he is said to have appointed military governors to Gulburga, Sāghar, and Dwārasamudra. It has been asserted that " the Hoysala (Ballāḷa III) does not figure in the organisation of the Mahrāṭṭa country by Mubārak, and the placing of the garrisons in the various forts along the Hoysala frontier, or in the subsequent invasion of Ma'bar by Khusru Khān." * The evidence of Ferishta is against this contention. 'The Sultān' says Ferishta, " stayed in that place (Dēvagiri), owing to the intervention of the rainy season. Having introduced changes in the country of Mahārāṣṭra, he built a mosque in the city of Dēvagiri which still remains. He placed military garrisons at Gulburga, Sāghar, Dwārasamudra and other places." † The appointment of a Mussalman governor to his capital compelled Ballāḷa III to hasten to Dwārasamudra, in order to repel the intruder. He was fortunate enough to defeat the enemy, and drive him away from his country. Two inscriptions dated in A. D. 1320, and 1321 respectively mention a minister of Ballāḷa called Mahāvīranāyakācāri Kaṭāri Sāḷuva Rāseya Nāyaka

* S. K. Iyengar: *South India and her Muhammadan Invaders*, p. 171.

† وسلطان بواسطۂ بارندگی آنجا توقف کرده ولایت مرہٹہ تصرف درآورده بشهر دیوگیر مسجدے
که بالفعل موجودست ساخته در گلبرگه و ساغر و دہور سمند و دیگر ممالک تھانہا نشاند

Tarikh-i-Ferishataāhi p. 125.

who destroyed the Turuka army. * As Ballāḷa III or his officers won no victories over the armies of Alā-ud-Din, and as the Tughlaks did not come into conflict with him until A. D. 1328, the victory of Rāseya Nāyaka should have been won over the officer whom Mubārak Khilji had posted to Dwārasamudra.

Ballāḷa seems to have remained in the north until 1320, when he led an army against the rāja of Kampili, but secured no substantial advantage. He returned to the Cōḷa country in the same year to direct the operations against the Pāṇḍyas in person, and took up his residence at Tiruvaṇṇāmalai. But his ally Vīra Pāṇḍya whom his army was assisting could not cope with the enemy. Samudra Pāṇḍya and his friend Parākrama marched upon Kannanūr and laid siege to it. There was some severe fighting on the occasion, when Singeya Daṇṇāyaka, son of Maiduna Sōmeya Daṇṇāyaka, a brother-in-law of Ballāḷa III was slain and the fort was ultimately captured. † Though the Pāṇḍyan victory blocked the progress of Ballāḷa's conquests in the Cōḷa country, it did not prevent him form re-establishing the Hoysala authority in Kongu. ‡ The campaign having come to an end, Ballāḷa broke up his camp at Tiruvaṇṇāmalai, and returned to Dōrasamudra in 1322, only to contemplate fresh schemes of conquest.

The small kingdom of Doravadi § on his north-eastern frontier had been the cause of considerable annoyance to Ballāḷa III ever since he ascended the throne. It was founded by Mummaḍi Singeya Nāyaka

* *MAR.* 1910, p. 35; *ibid* 1914 p.

† *MAR.* 1913. p. 41.

‡ His earliest dated inscription in Coimbatore bears the Śaka date 1245 corresponding to A. D., 1323 (*MER.* 588 of 1905).

§ See App. B, 'Note on Doravadi.'

who rose to prominence in the service of king Rāmadēva of Dēvagiri during the last quarter of the 13th century. Doravadi which Rāmadēva seems to have granted to him for his maintenance was included in the Ballakunde Three Hundred, * a district which was governed by a branch of the Siṇḍas in the past. Mummaḍi Singeya was ambitious and restless, and he soon picked up a quarrel with his neighbour Cavuṇḍarasa who was probably the Sēuṇa governor of the Nōlambavāḍi province. Cavuṇḍa placing himself at the head of his forces was proceeding against Doravadi, when he was opposed and killed by Mummaḍi Singeya in a battle. † This victory not only enhanced his reputation, but secured his freedom from the interference of provincial officers. It also gave him an opportunity to increase the extent of his kingdom. In the first place, he seized the territory of Cavuṇḍa extending as far as Harihara in the Dāvaṇagere tālūka in the west; secondly, he appropriated the estates of the petty chieftains who were in his neighbourhood. He raised an army and attacked '... mmalūrkallu' in the Hiriyūr tālūka in 1281; ‡ and he also fought during the same year with Sangaiya Nāyaka of Vētaṇḍakal and defeated him. § As a consequence of these victories, he became a powerful baron on the southern marches of the Sēuṇa kingdom.

Mummaḍi Singeya appears to have died sometime before 1300, and was succeeded by his son Khaṇḍeyarāya - Kampiladēva. One of the earliest acts of Kampiladēva was the restoration of the *agrahāra* of Harihara, which king Kṛṣṇakandhāra granted to Brāhmaṇs some two generations earlier. ¶ He invaded,

* *SII.* iv. 260.

† *EC.* vii. Ci. 24.

‡ *EC.* xi. Hr. 86.

§ *ibid.* Hk. 37.

¶ *ibid.* Dg. 26.

as mentioned already, the Hoysala kingdom in 1303, at the command of his sovereign Rāmadēva, and forced Ballāḷa III to retire from Banavāse.* Nothing more is known of his activity until 1309, when he built a temple in honour of Prasanna Virūpākṣa at Hampe.† The first stage in the reign of Kampiladēva may be said to have come to an end with this year.

During the next ten years, the principality of Doravadi had undergone important changes. The death of Rāmadēva and the subsequent disruption of the Sēuṇa kingdom offered an excellent opportunity for Kampiladēva not only to assert his independence, but to acquire fresh territory by seizing as much of the crumbling Sēuṇa kingdom as he could grasp. It was probably during these years that he pushed forward the eastern boundary of his state as far as Siruguppa in the Beḷḷāry tālūka. It is also possible that he conquered the districts on the northern bank of the Tungabhadra;‡ but no epigraphic evidence is available in support of this view. The rapidity with which his power had grown, seems to have alarmed

* *MAR.* 1913 p. 50.

† *LR.* 46; *VR.* 1, Bl. 335. This shrine is different from the famous Virūpākṣa temple which is certainly a more ancient foundation.

‡ ودر سنه هفت صد و نوزده (۷۱۹) که تمام ممالک محروسهٔ هندوستان را به تسخیر و تصرف در آورد - و خود بدکن آمده در استیصال کفره و تسخیر دیوگیر کوشیده تا بیجانگر که الحال بعضے بلاد تعلقهٔ او به کرناتک بیجاپور زبان زد است و راجه مستقل داشت تاخته مساجد ساخته؛ علاء الدین را از نو تعمیر نموده چندگاه سواد قلعهٔ دیوگیر پایۂ تخت خود ساخته مسمّی به دولت آباد گردانیده تمام متوطنانِ دہلی آباد کرده خود را قہراً وجبراً جلائے وطن نموده آنجا برده - چنانچه در ذکر سلاطینِ دہلی به تحریر آمده آباد ساخت.

Khāfi Khān: *Mumtakhab-al-lubāb* Part III p. 7. Bibliotheca Indica. (New series: 1389).

his neighbours, especially Ballāḷa III who could not countenance the birth of a powerful kingdom in his neighbourhood.

According to an inscription of Nagar dated 1320, Ballāḷa III "with all the troops of the armed force marched upon Kapiladēva." * The cause of this invasion is nowhere recorded. It is just possible that Ballāḷa had embarked upon this campaign with the object of rooting out an enemy while he had not yet become very formidable. Coupled with this, he might have also been actuated by a desire to annex the region which formed an integral part of the Hoysala dominions in the past. Whatever might be his motive, he managed to lead his army to the very heart of the enemy's kingdom, and lay encamped in the vicinity of his capital. Kampila, thereupon, came marching 'with all his armed force,' 'and both armies were drawn up facing each other.' In the battle that followed, some of the Hoysala officers were killed, and Ballāḷa was defeated. † An undated epigraph from Kūḍli in the Ṣīmoga district refers to another encounter between the two chiefs. It is said that Ballāḷa who wanted to destroy the pride of Kampila, "went with speed on Siraguppe, and encamped there." 'Kampila went out to meet the enemy,' and 'fought with his army so as to win the praise of all the world!' ‡ The result of this battle was not very different from that of the last. Ballāḷa III and Kampila appear to have met on the battle-field for the last time in 1325. § As the inscription recording the event is in a damaged condition, it cannot be definitely ascertained how the battle ended. Rice's translation would have us believe that

* *EC.* viii. Nr. 19. † *ibid.*

‡ *MAR.* 1923, 121. § *EC.* xii. Tp. 24.

Kampila was slain; but there are strong reasons for doubting the accuracy of his translation. Owing to the peeling off of the stone, several letters between the words Kampila and '*modala niṟudu kondu*' have disappeared. The translation, therefore, cannot be depended on. Again, according to the Muhammadan historians, Kampila was alive until 1327, when he was slain by K͟hwāja Jahān who invaded his kingdom. * If it be true that Kampila died at the hands of the Mussalmans, his death could not have taken place in a battle two years earlier. Therefore, it may be stated that the last campaign of Ballāḷa III also ended as undecisively as its predecessors.

While the struggle between Ballāḷa III and Kampila was still undecided, the Muhammadan invaders from the north made their appearance once again. The Tughlak Sultāns proved more dangerous to the stability of the South Indian Hindu kingdoms than their predecessors. The kingdom of Warrangal was overthrown in 1323, and Telingāṇa became a province of Delhi; at the same time Orissa was attacked, and the authority of the Sultān was established in Ma'bar. Ghiās-ud-Din, the first ruler of the Tughlak dynasty died in 1325, and was succeeded by his son, Muhammad bin Tughlak. † It was during the early years of the reign of this monarch that an expedition was sent against the kingdom of Kampila. The invasion was not caused by the desire of the Sultān to conquer more territory. He had a cousin called Bahā-ud-Din Gurshāsp, ‡ who rose up in rebellion against

* *ED.* iii. p. 615.

† Barnī: *ED.* iii pp. 231-235.

‡ He is also called Bahādar Gurshāsp:

ملک بهادر گرشاسپ عارض لشکر در سفر بلغاک کرد۔ *Tārikh-i-Mubārak Shāhi* p. 99.

him in 1327. Having been defeated in battle by the army of the Sultān, he fled from Deccan, and sought the protection of Kampiladēva, who gave him shelter, and treated him with consideration becoming his rank. The Sultān himself arrived at Dēvagiri, and despatched an army under Khwāja Jahān to bring back the fugitive. They marched upon Kampila's capital and laid siege to it. He held out for a while ; but soon realising that the fort would have to be surrendered owing to the shortage of the supplies, he made up his mind to do everything in his power to save Bahā-ud-Din from the wrath of the Sultān. He sent him with an escort to the court of Ballāḷa III, hoping probably that it would not be possible for the Sultān to capture him easily. Kampila did not entertain any thought of surrender. He issued a command to all the women of the palace to burn themselves alive ; when that was done, he had the gates of the fort thrown open and sallied forth to meet the Sultān's army. He and his followers fought with the besiegers bravely, until they fell dead. The town was captured, and several inhabitants including the eleven sons of Kampila were made prisoners. The sons of Kampila embraced Islam, on account of which the Sultān made them *amīrs*, and treated them courteously. The kingdom of Kampila was annexed to the empire of Delhi. *

Khwāja Jahān next proceeded against Ballāḷa III who was then sheltering Bahā-ud-Din. Ballāḷa, however, had no desire to court trouble for considerations of chivalry. As soon as he heard that the Muhammadan army was advancing upon his capital, he seized Bahā-ud-Din, and sent him bound to Khwāja Jahān, acknowledging at the same time the supremacy of the

* *ED.* iii p. 615.

Sultān. Ballāḷa III, by following a prudent policy, averted a disaster which otherwise would have destroyed his kingdom.

The kingdom of Kampila which was annexed by the Sultān did not remain as a province of his empire for long. Although information is totally lacking regarding its affairs during the succeeding years, it is definitely known, on the authority of the contemporary writers, that sometime before 1343, the Sultān appointed a relation of Kanya Nāyak of Warrangal, who embraced Islam, as the governor of the province; but the governor soon apostatised from Islam and asserted his independence. *

The foregoing description of the events of the reign of Ballāḷa III makes it clear that the northern frontier of his kingdom corresponded roughly to the northern boundary of the present Mysore state. The region corresponding to the districts of North Canara, Dhārwār, Bijāpūr, Gulburga and Nellore was never included in Ballāḷa's kingdom. Therefore, he could not have appointed officers to defend the territory which lay outside his dominions.

Was the Hoysala kingdom exposed to the attacks of the Bahmani Sultāns? and were the founders of Vijayanagara employed by Ballāḷa III 'to stem the new flood of Bahmani invasion?' It is true that Harihara I and his brother Bukka are referred to in the *Burhān-i-ma'asir* as the rulers of the country beyond the southern boundary of the kingdom which Alā-ud-Din Hasan Bahmani had established. † The evidence of *Burhān-i-ma'asir* is confirmed by Ibn Battūta, and the inscriptions. According to Battūta,

* *ED.* iii. p. 245.

† *IA.* xxviii p. 148.

Sultān Jamāl-ad-Din of Honawar was 'under the suzerainty of an infidel Sultān named Haryab'; * and Haryab has been correctly identified with Hariappa or Harihara I, whose sway, as shown by an epigraph dated 1339 A. D. at Bādāmi, † extended over the Bijāpūr district. Since the reign of Harihara I lasted until 1356, it is quite likely that he should have come into conflict with Alā-ud-Din Hasan; but it is absolutely certain that Ballāḷa III had nothing to do with this conflict; for, in the first place, the founders of Vijayanagara, as shown already, had no connection whatever with Ballāḷa III; and secondly, the Bahmani kingdom did not come into existence during the life-time of Ballāḷa. Alā-ud-Din Hasan founded the Bahmani kingdom in 1347, whereas Ballāḷa III died in the middle of 1342. ‡ How could the Hoysala dominions have become exposed to the invasions of the Bahmani Sultāns, some twenty years before the birth of the Bahmani kingdom.? It is highly improbable that Ballāḷa III could have provided in 1328 against a danger which was still in the womb of the future. Therefore, the statement that Ballāḷa III posted the founders of Vijayanagara at important places along his northern frontier to stem the tide of the Bahmani invasions need not be taken seriously.

Section 4:—The belief that Ballāḷa III enthroned Harihara I at Vijayanagara is not based on evidence. It is stated that in the later years of his reign, Ballāḷa III "had not a fixed residence as his predecessors, but he frequently changed his capital according to the needs of the empire, and in order to secure

* Ibn Battūta: *Travels in Asia and Africa*, (The Broadway Travellers). p. 230.

† *IA*. x. p. 63. ‡ *EC*. vi. Kd. 75.

its defence against the Mussalmans. * The capital was changed for the first time in 1328. Ballāḷa shifted the capital of his kingdom from Dōrasamudra to Uṇṇāmalepaṭṭaṇa. Two years later, he went to

* Heras: *The Beginnings*, p. 65.

It is not true that the predecessors of Ballāḷa III had a fixed residence (*neleviḍu*). That they were in the habit of changing their residence frequently is shown by the schedule given below:

Reference.	Year.	King.	Neleviḍu.
EC. v Bl. 58 ...	S. 1039	Viṣṇuvardhana ...	Vēlāpura.
EC. v Mj. 60 ...	About S. 1120	Vīra Ganga Viṣṇuvardhana ...	Bēlāpura.
EC. iv Kr. 78 ...	About S. 1130	Viṣṇuvardhana ...	Bankāpura.
EC. v Bl. 124 ...	S. 1055	do. ...	do.
EC. v Ak. 144 ...	S. 1059	do. ...	Bankāpura and Tāḷavanapura.
EC. v Cn. 199 ...	Siddhārthi S. 1061	Vīra Ganga Viṣṇuvardhana ...	Bankāpura.
EC. v Ak. 18 ...	do.	Viṣṇuvardhana ...	do.
EC. v Ak. 52 ...	S. 1073	Narasimha ...	do.
EC. v Bl. 77 ...	S. 1120	Ballāḷa ...	Kukkanūr-Koppa.
EC. iv Ng. 47 ...	S. 1121	do. ...	Lokkiguṇḍi.
EC. v Cn. 172 ...	S. 1131	do. ...	Vijayasamudra.
EC. iii Nj. 36 ...	S. 1151	Sōmēśwara ...	Kannanūr.
EC. iv Kr. 63 ...	S. 1159	do. ...	Pāṇḍyamaṇḍala.
EC. iii TN. 103 ...	S. 1161	do. ...	Cōḷa Rājya.
MAR. 1923. No. 46 ...		do. ...	Dōcalabiḍu.
EC. v Cn. 203 ...		do. ...	Varadaṇakuppa.
MAR. 1918 ...		do. ...	Vijayarājēndra pattaṇa.

N. B.—The list is not exhaustive.

Vijayanagara where he remained until 1340. During the middle of this period, Ballāḷa enthroned Harihara as his *mahāmaṇḍalēśvara* in the north". This is said to be proved by the mutual understanding that existed between "the emperor and his *mahāmaṇḍalēśvara*", as shown by the following:—

Harihara fortified Bārakūru in	...	1336
Ballāḷa III paid a visit to inspect Harihara's work in ...	...	1338
Ballāḷa III was at Vijayanagara in	...	1339
Cāmarāja, a subordinate of Harihara built the fort of Bādāmi in	...	1340

It is true that Ballāḷa III frequently changed his residence during the later years of his reign in accordance with the administrative needs of his kingdom. That, however, should not be taken as an indication of the change of the capital. Dōrasamudra remained the capital of Ballāḷa's kingdom until the very last. * The various *nelevīḍus* mentioned in his inscriptions should be regarded as temporary camps, where he happened to be staying for some reason or other. It is not true that Ballāḷa transferred his residence to Tiruvaṇṇāmalai for the first time in 1328; for, he was there already for two years during 1321-22. † His visit to the place in 1328 must have been due to the outbreak of war on his southern frontier. He returned to the north in 1330, and remained for a short time at Virūpākṣapaṭṭaṇa (Virūpapura) in the Magdi tālūka, not Vijayanagara. He did not stay here until 1340, but went to Hosabeṭṭa in 1333 and Dōrasamudra in 1335, returning to Virūpākṣapura in 1339. He was at Dōrasamudra once

* *Kampili and Vijayanagara*, p. 23.   † *EC.* iv. Gu. 69, 85.

L

again in 1340, * where he performed the *abhiṣēka* of his son, before departing to the south for conducting his final campaign against the Sultān of Madura. There is absolutely no evidence in support of the statement that he enthroned Harihara in 1336, or at any other time. Therefore, it should be dismissed as a speculation completely emancipated from the wholesome control of facts. The unity that is supposed to have existed between the ideals and plans of Ballāḷa III and Harihara must also be regarded as imaginary. There is no evidence to show that Harihara I ever built a fort at Bārakūru in 1336 ; and Ballāḷa's visit to that place in 1338, was due to a desire to encourage his troops stationed in the place to defend it against Harihara's attacks. As Ballāḷa III had nothing to do with the affairs of the kingdom of Vijayanagara, he could have had no connection direct or indirect with the construction of the fort of Bādāmi in 1339.

* *Kampili and Vijayanagara*, p. 23.

CHAPTER II.

THE EARLY HISTORY OF THE SANGAMA FAMILY.

Section 1 :—The true origin of the kingdom of Vijayanagara is revealed by an investigation of the contemporary records, Hindu as well as Muhammadan. The kingdom of Vijayanagara seems to have sprung up from the principality of Doravadi or Kambīla, as it was known to the Muhammadan historians, which Sultān Muhammad destroyed in 1327. * The destruction of this state is vividly described by Ibn Battūta who came to India in 1333. As he became intimately acquainted with the sons of Kampiladēva who embraced Islam subsequent to the death of their father, he would have gathered all his information regarding the circumstances under which Kampiladēva died from eye-witnesses who participated in the fight. Therefore, his account of the siege and capture of Kampiladēva's capital is of special importance.

"Sultān Tughalik," says he, "had a nephew, son of his sister, named Bahā-ud-Din Gushtāsp whom he made governor of a province... And when his uncle was dead he refused to give his oath to the late

* و در سنه سبع و عشرین و سبعمائة (۷۲۷) سلطان محمود عزیمت دیوگیر کرد و هم در آخر سال مذکور ملک بهادر گرشاسپ عارض لشکر در ساغر یلغار کرد. سلطان خواجهٔ جهان را با عساکر قاهره بجهت قهر او نامزد فرمود. چون خواجهٔ جهان آنجا رسید بهادر مذکور با مقدار جمعیتهٔ خویش پیش آمد و بجنگ پیوست. آخر الامر طاقت نیاورد و منهزم شده بدست هندوان اسیر و دستگیر گشت.

Tārikh-i-Mubārak Shāhi p. 99.

Sultān's son and successor. The Sultān sent a force against him, . . . there was a fierce battle, . . . and the Sultān's troops gained victory. Bahā-ud-Din fled to one of the Hindu princes, the rāi of Kambīla. . . . This prince had territories situated among inaccessible mountains, and was one of the chief princes of the infidels.

"When Bahā-ud-Din made his escape to this prince, he was pursued by the soldiers of the Sultān of India, who surrounded the rāi's territories. The infidel saw his danger, for his stores of grain were exhausted and his great fear was that the enemy would carry off his person by force; so he said to Bahā-ud-Din, 'Thou seest how we are situated. I am resolved to die with my family, and with all who will imitate me. Go to such and such a prince (naming a Hindu prince), and stay with him; he will defend thee.' He sent some one to conduct him thither. Then he commanded a great fire to be prepared and lighted. Then he burned his furniture and said to his wives and daughters, 'I am going to die, and such of you as prefer it, do the same.' Then it was seen that each one of these women washed herself, rubbed her body with sandal-wood, kissed the ground before the rāi of Kambīla, and threw herself upon the pile. All perished. The wives of his nobles, ministers, and chief men imitated them, and other women also did the same.

"The rāi, in his turn, washed, rubbed himself with sandal, and took his arms, but did not put on his breastplate. Those of his men who resolved to die with him, followed his example. They sallied forth to meet the troops of the Sultān and fought till every-one of them fell dead. The town was taken, its inhabitants were made prisoners, and eleven sons of the rāi were made prisoners and carried to the Sultān who made them all Mussalmans." *

What happened in the kingdom of Kambīla, immediately after the death of the rāi is nowhere related. The historian Zia-ud-Din Barnī, one of the companions of Sultān Muhammad mentions Kambīla as one of the provinces included in the empire of Delhi. He casually states that the government of the province was entrusted to the care of a Hindu who embraced Muhammadanism. While narrating the events connected with the rebellion at Sannām and Sāmāna which broke out in 1344, Barnī observes:

"While this was going on, a revolt broke out among the Hindus at Arangal. Kanya Nāyak had gathered strength in the country. Malik Makbūl, the *nāib-wazīr*, fled to Delhi, and the Hindus took possession of Arangal, which was thus entirely lost. About the same time, one of the relations of Kanya Nāyak whom the Sultān had sent to Kambala, apostatised from Islam and stirred up a revolt. The land of Kambala also was thus lost, and fell into the hands of the Hindus." †

It is evident from these two extracts that the government of the kingdom of Kambīla, which was destroyed in 1327, was entrusted by the Sultān to a relation of Kanya Nāyak of Warrangal who embraced Islam. But this person, having apostatised from his adopted faith, reverted to Hinduism, and by stirring up a rebellion, asserted his independence in or about 1344 A. D.

* *ED.* iii. pp. 614-15. † *ibid* pp. 245-6.

The name of the relation of Kanya Nāyak who successfully headed the rebellion of Kambīla against the Sultān is nowhere disclosed. It is, however, possible to discover his name by an investigation of the inscriptions belonging to this period. Judging from the position of Kambīla as described by the Mussalman historians, it should have extended from the Southern frontier of the province of Dēvagiri to Kampili on the Tungabhadra from which its name is evidently derived. * Who was the prince or king that was ruling this region from 1327 to 1344? It is stated in the Kāpalūr plates dated 1335 that Harihara, son of Sangama, a descendant of Yadu, was ruling this part of the country from his capital Kuñjarakōna on the Tungabhadra. † The same information is conveyed by another grant dated in the same year coming from the Bāgēpalli tāluka of the Kōlār district. ‡ As these grants are declared spurious, the value of their evidence has become vitiated, and they cannot be of much use in the present discussion. There are other genuine records which should be considered in this context. It is stated in an epigraph of Aṭakalaguṇḍa in the Kurnool district that Harihara I was ruling this part of the country in 1339 from his *nelevīḍu* at Gutti. § According to an inscription dated 1340, the country round Bādāmi in the Bijāpūr district was governed by king Harihara. He bore the titles *mahāmaṇḍalēśvara, arirāyavibhāḷa, bhāshagetappuva - rāyara - gaṇḍa, and pūrvapaścima samudrādhipati.* ¶ It is stated in an unpublished inscription of the same date coming from the Kurnool district that Harihara was ruling the country in the neighbourhood

* *Mumtakab-al-lubāb.* Part iii. p. 7.

† *NDI.* i. Cp. 15.

‡ *EC.* x. Bg. 70.

§ *LR.* Vol. 23: pp. 52-53.

¶ *IA.* x. p. 6.

of the Śrīśaila mountain. * This is confirmed by a third inscription dated 1344, according to which Harihara's brother Bukka was ruling from Vidyānagara. † By 1342, the authority of Harihara was recognised on the coast of Konkan. Ibn Battūta who visited Konkan in 1342, states that Jamāl-ad-Din, the Sultān of Honawar, was the subordinate of a Hindu king called Haryab, ‡ who has been identified with Hariyappa or Harihara I of Vijayanagara.

The evidence of the inscriptions and Battūta make it clear that at least from 1339 Harihara I was governing the country over which Kampiladēva ruled before 1327. It should be borne in mind that this country was included, according to Barnī, in the dominions of the Sultān of Delhi until 1344, when, owing to the successful rebellion of its governor, it became independent. It follows from this that Harihara I of Vijayanagara and the Sultān of Delhi were holding sway over this region simultaneously between 1339 and 1344. This could not have happened if both of them were independent monarchs. It could have been only possible, if one of them chanced to be a subordinate of the other. Of the two, the Sultān of Delhi could not have been a subordinate of Harihara. Therefore, Harihara should have been a subordinate of the Sultān. As he was ruling the territories of the old kingdom of Kambīla about 1340, as a subordinate of the Sultān of Delhi, he should have been that relation of Kanya Nāyak whom the Sultān appointed as the governor of Kambīla sometime before 1344, but who stirred up in that year a rebellion against his

* *Mac. Mss.* 15-5-33. pp. 307-14.

† *EC.* x. Mb. 158. Sewell: *Historical Inscriptions* p. 189, 1.

‡ Ibn Battūta: *Travels in Asia and Africa,* (Broadway Travellers) p. 230.

master, and asserted his independence. Harihara appears to have been a follower of Islam at the time of his appointment to the governorship; but he soon abandoned it, and reverted to the faith of his fathers. * His reconversion to Hinduism which was the first act of his rebellion might have been actuated by considerations not purely religious. Probably the rebellion which was in essence a Hindu protest against the aggressive onslaughts of Islam could not have been as successful as it was but for Harihara's reconversion.

Section 2:—Who was this Harihara? Very little is known of the origin and the early history of his family. Though the information on the subject is very scanty, some attempts have already been made to reconstruct the story of his ancestors. It is said that Harihara's family was connected with the Kadambas of Banavāse. † A passage from Nikitin is cited in support of this statement: "The Hindu Sultān, Kadam," says he, "is a very powerful prince. He possesses a numerous army, and resides on a mountain at Bicheneghar." ‡ The word 'Kadam' in this passage is the name of the Vijayanagara king, and not of his family. Therefore, there is no reason to suppose that the ancestors of Harihara had any

* It is interesting to note that Bukka I, the younger brother of Harihara had a Muhammadan son. An imperfectly dated inscription from Ṣimoga (Ci. 65,) mentions Gengu Salār, son of Bukkaṇa Voḍeyar. The date of the inscription as engraved is *Śakavarṣa sahasrada Vikrama varṣada.* The expression *sahasrada* means, 'one thousand and'; and it is evident that the engraver had omitted something after 'and'. Bl. 3, dated about 1397, refers to the rebuilding of the *gōpura* at Bēlūr which Ganga Salār, the Turuka of Kallubarage had come and burnt. The Ganga Salār mentioned in Bl. 3, appears to be the same as the Ganga Salār of Ci. 65, for the names of these two persons agree; and they lived about the same time. It is not unlikely that Bukkaṇa Voḍeyar had a son who was a Muhammadan.

† Heras: *The Beginnings* p. 65.

‡ Nikitin: *India in the Sixteenth Century*: (Hok. Soc.) p. 29.

connection with the Kadambas of Banavāse or any other place. Again, it is suggested that 'the ancestors of the first dynasty of Vijayanagara were the members of the famous family of Kēśavadaṇḍanātha,' * who was one of the officers of Ballāḷa II. Three arguments are brought forward in support of this contention :—

(1) Kēśavadaṇḍanātha's family is 'the only Yādava family found in the inscriptions besides the ruling family of the Hoysalas'. And Harihara and his brothers trace their descent from the same family. (2) Kēśavadaṇḍanātha's family, 'just as the family of Sangama', is called a 'Karṇāṭa family.' (3) Several names of the members of one family resemble those of the other. †

None of these arguments can establish the connection of the family of Harihara with that of Kēśavadaṇḍanātha. In the first place, Kēśava's family was not the only one besides the Hoysalas to claim descent from the mythical hero, Yadu. The Sēuṇas of Dēvagiri, the Yādavarāyas of Candragiri, ‡ and the Pāṇḍyas of Ucchangi claimed a similar descent. Therefore, the ancestors of Harihara may be said to have been connected with any one of them. Secondly, there is no justification for calling Harihara's family a 'Karṇāṭa family.' It is, no doubt, true that in one inscription, Sangama, the father of Harihara is said to have enabled the Lakṣmi of Karṇāṭa *dēśa* to wear her ear-rings ; §

* Heras : *The Biginnings* p. 76. † *ibid.* pp. 75-76.

‡ *T. T. Dēvasthānam Inscriptions.* Vol. I p. 101. Sāyaṇa's *Subhāṣita : Rāja Cāṭupaddhati* : Md. Gov. Or. Mss. Lb.

Sindhuś-candrasya bandhur-vanam-idam-api-tallakṣma sāraṅga kīrṇam
Śailēyāc-candrakāntādadhati na rajani pālayētvām tadīyā
Bhūpam Śrī Ranganātham Yadukula-tilakam bhavya-hētōḥ bhajēta
Brūtē vidvēṣi-yoṣin nijapatim-abhajat-bhīti-mai jāta-nītim. ‖

§ *EC.* viii *TL.* 206 ; Nr. 69 ; xii Pg. 69.

M

but this cannot be taken to mean that Sangama and therefore his son belonged to a family called the 'Karṇāṭa family.' What all we can say with reason is that Sangama ruled somewhere in the Karṇāṭa country; but that is a different proposition. The mere fact that the families of Kēśavadaṇḍanātha and Harihara ruled in Karṇāṭa, does not unite them, making them thereby a single family. Lastly, similarity of names cannot be taken as a serious argument, since such similarity may be discovered between the names of several other families of the time. Therefore the suggested connection between the families of Kēśavadaṇḍanātha and Harihara should be considered improbable; and if it is necessary to discover the origin of the family of Harihara, an attempt should be made to explore sources other than those mentioned above.

The inscriptions of Harihara I and his successors yield some information, though scanty, about his father and grandfather. The name of his father was Sangama, and he is said to have been a powerful chief, though nothing definite is known about his achievements. * The father of Sangama was a chief called Bukka who is occasionally mentioned in the records of his descendants. † An epigraph dated 1314 A.D. coming from

* However, in a copper-plate grant attributed to King Harihara II, (*MAR.* 1918, p. 50) some of his exploits are enumerated. "He performed the sixteen great gifts in Rāmēśvaram and other holy places. Quickly damming the Kāvēri when in full flood, he crossed over, and seizing the enemy alive, took possession of his Tañca kingdom (Tanjore) and the city of Śrīrangapaṭṭaṇa. He conquered Cēra, Cōḷa, and Pāṇḍya and together with the lord of Madura Mānabhūṣa, the Turuṣka, and the Gajapati king." The inscription in which this passage occurs is a forgery of the 16th century; for, (1) the passage is bodily taken from the *praśasti* of the Tuḷuva kings describing the campaigns of Narasa Nāyaka; and (2) it does not occur in the *praśasti* of the First Dynasty in any inscription excepting the present. Therefore, Sangama may be said to have become famous, only on account of his sons; but for them his name would not have come down to posterity.

† *NDI.* i. Cp. 15; *EC.* x. Gd. 46; MB. 158.

Gōzalavīḍu in the Kanigiri tālūka of the Nellore district mentions a Bukkarāya Voḍayalu bearing the titles of *samasta bhuvanāśraya, pañcamahāśabda, maṇḍalēśvara, mūrurāyara-gaṇḍa, arirāya vibhāḷa, bhāṣadappuvarāya-gaṇḍa, navakhaṇḍa pṛthvīśvara, and Vīrūpākṣadēva divya śrī pādapadmārādhaka.* * It must be noted that the first three titles were never made use of by the Vijayanagara kings; the third is especially interesting, as it denotes that Bukkarāya Voḍayalu was an ordinary chief, a mere *maṇḍalēśvara.* Therefore, the inscription certainly belongs to a period anterior to the establishment of the kingdom of Vijayanagara; and the titles, *arirāya vibhāḷa, bhāṣadappuvarāya-gaṇḍa, Virūpākṣadēva divya śrī pādapadmārādhaka* which are peculiar to the descendants of Sangama, point out that this Bukkarāya Voḍayalu should have also been a member of the family. Having these titles and the date of the inscription in view, it is not possible to avoid the conclusion that Bukkarāya Voḍayalu mentioned therein is the same as the father of Sangama referred to above. †

* *NDI.* ii. Kg. 7.

† The identification was made 27 years ago by Messrs. Butterworth and Vēṇugōpāla Ceṭṭy in the last volume of the *Nellore District Inscriptions*, p. 1467. But the Rev. Fr. Heras does not agree with them. "Messrs. Butterworth and Vēṇugōpāla Ceṭṭy *with the preconceived idea* that all the Vijayanagara dynasties are Telugu, are inclined to identify Sangama's father with a chief named Bukkarāya Oḍayalu who receives several honorific titles in an inscription at the Nellore district." "But the father of this Bukkarāya Oḍayalu seems to be a Reḍḍi chief." *The Beginnings.* p. 74.

If Fr. Heras had studied the question calmly, he would have agreed with Messrs. Butterworth and Vēṇugōpāla Ceṭṭy. The inscription does not mention the father of this 'Bukkarāya Oḍayalu' at all. However, it mentions the donor Gangi Reḍḍi of Iḍumakanṭi family, and his parents, Peddi Reḍḍi and Cānasāni. The text of the inscription runs thus :—
స్వస్తి సమస్తభువనా(శయ పంచమహాశబ్ద మండలేశ్వర మూరురాయరగండ
అరిరాయవిభాళ భాషదప్పువరాయగండ నవఖండపృథ్వీశ్వర విరూపాక్షదేవ
దివ్య శ్రీపాదపద్మారాధకులైన శ్రీబుక్కరాయఒడయల బట (డం) యినమ

Therefore, the present grant makes it quite clear that Bukka, the grandfather of Harihara I, was holding sway about A. D. 1314 over a portion of the Nellore district. It is a matter of common knowledge that this region formed part of the Kākatīya kingdom which Muhammad bin Tughlak had overthrown in 1323 A. D. Pratāparudra II, who had been liberated from his imprisonment by some of his officers, exercised some sort of authority over this part of his kingdom until 1330. Bukkarāya Voḍayalu of the Gōzalaviḍu inscription should have been a subordinate of Pratāparudra II.

The information gleaned from the inscriptions and the contemporary writers about the ancestors of Harihara I may be summarised in a few sentences. His grandfather, Bukkarāya Voḍayalu was holding sway over a portion of the Nellore district as a subordinate of Pratāparudra II about 1314 A.D. Nothing, however, is known about his father Sangama except that he begot five sons who established the kingdom of

కంటి గంగిరెడ్డిం గారు స్వస్తి శ్రీశకవర్షంబులు ౧౨౩౬ అగునేటి ఆనంద సంవత్సర వైశాఖ ౫ గు॥ తండ్రి పెద్దిరెడ్డికిని తల్లి చానసానికిని &c. It has been correctly rendered into English by Messrs. Butterworth and Vēṇugōpāla Ceṭṭy: "Iḍumakanṭi Gangi Reḍḍi Gāru the servant of (Hail) Bukkarāya Voḍayalu . . . gave . . . for the religious merit of his (Gangi Reḍḍi's) father Peddi Reḍḍi and his mother Cānasāni &c." It is not known how Fr. Heras got the idea that Bukkarāya Voḍayalu's father was a 'Reḍḍi chief' at any rate, he could not have been indebted to the text of the inscription which is quite clear on the point. Another writer attempts to identify Bukkarāya Voḍayalu of the inscription with Bukka I. "The fact of Bukka I's patronage to a Telugu poet or even of his having under him a Telugu governor—Iḍumakanṭi Gangi Reḍḍi Gāru in Śaka 1314 (Butterworth, Nellore Inscriptions ii, p. 643) does not necessarily mean that Bukka was of Telugu origin." (*Jr. Bom. Hist. Soc.* Vol. ii p. 117). The identification is wrong; for, in the first place, the date of the inscription is Śaka 1236, and not Śaka 1314. Secondly, Bukka I died about Śaka 1300; therefore, he could not be reigning in Śaka 1314, some fourteen years after his death. If the inscription did really belong to a subordinate of Bukka I, then it establishes that he was of Telugu origin; since, ruling as he did in Śaka 1236, in Nellore, he should have been a subordinate of the Kākatīya king, Pratāparudra II.

Vijayanagara. Harihara I, the eldest of Sangama's sons, was related to Kanya Nāyak who began to rule at Warrangal in 1344. He embraced Islam some years before that date, and was consequently appointed by Muhammad bin Tughlak as the governor of the kingdom of Kampila which he overthrew in 1327. He ruled his province at first from Kuñjarakōna, and subsequently from Vijayanagara. He reverted to Hinduism sometime before 1344, and stirring up a revolt against the Sultān, became independent.

CHAPTER III.

THE KĀKATĪYAS AND THE FOUNDERS OF VIJAYANAGARA

Section 1:—The connection of the founders of Vijayanagara with the Kākatīyas suggested in the previous chapter, is also shown though indirectly by the crest of the kings of Vijayanagara as well as some features of their administrative system.

The Crest.—It is well-known that '*varāha*' or the boar was the crest of the four dynasties that ruled over Vijayanagara. What was the source from which they obtained it? The boar crest was at first made use of by the Cāḷukyas of Bādāmi; and it was inherited from them by all the branches of the family, who adopted it, with a few modifications. The Cāḷukyas of Kalyāṇi who established a wide-spread empire in the Deccan made the boar crest the symbol of their imperial power. The feudatory families which recognised their overlordship were profoundly influenced by the manners of their court and methods of administration. All of them copied the ways of their sovereigns; they even modelled their *praśastis* on that of the royal family. The Kākatīyas seem to have gone a step further; they adopted also the royal crest.

After the fall of the Cāḷukyas, the three monarchies which stepped into their place fostered the old administrative institutions with a few changes here and there. But the old royal crest disappeared everywhere except in Teliṅgāṇa. The Sēuṇas made use of the Garuḍa crest, and the Hoysalas, the tiger. The Kākatīyas alone had shown respect to the Cāḷukyan boar. It is mentioned for the first time in the inscriptions of Prōla II. He is said to have marked the breast of his enemy, Guṇḍa of Mantrakūṭa "with the sign of a boar." * The image of the Kākatīya boar is also found engraved on the seals of the copper-plates of Gaṇapati; † and it is also engraved at the top of some of the stone inscriptions of Pratāparudra II. ‡

The founders of Vijayanagara should, therefore, have borrowed their crest only from the Kākatīyas, for no other royal house made use of it at the time of the birth of the new kingdom. One peculiarity which is common to the Kākatīya and Vijayanagara crests establishes, in our view, the connection between them more firmly. On the seals attached to the inscriptions of Gaṇapati and Pratāparudra II, the figure of a dagger is engraved in front of the boar; the dagger is also carved on the Vijayanagara seals, but in a slightly different manner. Whereas the dagger in the Kākatīya seals is made to stand on its hilt, its position is reversed in the Vijayanagara seals, where it is made to stand on the point. Notwithstanding this small difference, it may be confidently asserted that the founders of Vijayanagara were indebted to the Kākatīyas for their crest.

Section 2:—The Administrative Features:—The founders of Vijayanagara seem to have modelled their administrative machinery to some extent on that of the Kākatīyas. (*a*) The administrative divisions that were in vogue in the Vijayanagara kingdom were either copied or evolved from those obtaining in the dominions of the Kākatīyas. The village served as the foundation

* *IA.* x. p. 17. † *EI.* xviii. See the plate opposite to p. 351.

‡ It is engraved on the top of an inscription at Nandalūr by the side of the eastern *gōpura* of the Cokkanāthaswāmi temple.

on which the whole fabric rested. A few villages were grouped together to form what was known as *sthala*. A few *sthalas* constituted a *nāḍu*; a few *nāḍus* formed a *sīma*; and a few *sīmas* became a *rājya*. This system of grouping the divisions of administration was not entirely created by Harihara I or his successors. What they had done was only to bring the scattered elements which they found existing under a system. The *sthala* and the *rājya** are occasionally met with in the Hoysala and the Sēuṇa inscriptions; but they do not seem to connote artificial sub-divisions of territory created for the sake of administrative convenience. There is reason to believe that the Kākatīya monarchs, especially Rudrāmbā and Pratāparudra, made a conscious effort to overhaul the administrative machinery of their kingdom. An examination of the lithic records of their time reveals the existence of administrative divisions that bear a close kinship to those obtaining under Vijayanagara. The *sthala* may be taken up for consideration at first:—

Reference.	Date.	Name of the *sthala*.
NDI. O. 139 ...	1218-19	Nellore.
„ P. 37 ...	„	Paḍiyāla.
Teliṅgāṇa Inscriptions, Kākatīya. No. 34 ..	1267	Pānuganṭi.
NDI. D. 1 ...	1272-73	Pōligaṇḍa.
„ D. 72 ..	1272-73	Addanki.
„ D. 101 ...	1273-74	Arulūru. Peṇḍlūru.

* The names of the *rājyas* of Niḍugal, Kundāṇi and Sētu are met with in the inscriptions of Ballāḷa III. These were independent kingdoms which he inherited or conquered. After their acquisition by Ballāḷa III, in spite of the fact that they had a common ruler, they were still spoken of as *rājyas*, owing probably to the force of habit. They were in no sense artificial units of territory created for administrative purposes.

Reference.	Date.	Name of the *sthala*.
MER. 285 of 1893 SII. IV No. 1152. ...	1278	(?)
NDI. O. 53 ..	1293-4	Ravinūtala.
„ O. 129 ...	1293-4	Ravinūtala.
MER. 565 of 1909 ...	1299	{ Gurimadala, Pingaḷa.
„ A. 10 of 1918. 19.	1303	Nandyāla.
NDI. O. 54 ...	1306	Cadalavāḍa.
MER. 715 of 1921 ...	1317	Koṇḍūri.
NDI. Kr. 28 ...	1328-29	Pūngināṭi.

The artificial character of the *sthalas* is brought out clearly by two facts : (*a*) Each *sthala* was a group consisting of a few villages. O. 101 refers to 8 villages included in the *sthalas* of Aralūru and Peṇḍlūru. MER. 715 of 1921 alludes to 18 villages of Koṇḍūri *sthala*. (*b*) Each *sthala* was an artificial division created to suit administrative convenience. It was placed in charge of an officer sometimes called a *sādhvaka*. D. 72 mentions the *sādhyaka* of the *sthala* of Addanki. O. 139 refers to the ruler of the Nellore *sthala*. The Telingāṇa inscription (Kākatīya No. 34) refers to the ruler of the Pānuganṭi *sthala*.

In some parts of the kingdom, in the place of the *sthala*, we meet with the *kampaṇa* :—

Reference.	Date.	Name of *kampaṇa*.
NDI. U. 48 ..	1252-3	Cilukapāḍu.
„ D. 25 ..	1254-5	Amavakalamāri.
„ D. 28 ...	1254-5	Amavankalamārī.

Over the *sthala* and the *kampaṇa* was the *nāḍu* :—

Reference.		Date.	Name of the *nāḍu*.
NDI.	O. 139 ...	1218-19	Pāka.
MER.	196 of 1905 ...	1260	Kamma. Pūngi.
„	333 of 1915 ...	1277	Anumakoṇḍa.
„	406 of 1911 ...	1287	Pottapi. Mulki Paruva.
NDI.	O. 129 ...	1293-94	Kamma.
	O. 53 ...	1293-94	do.
	Kr. 1 ...	1315-16	Pūngi.
	Kr. 23 ...	„	do.
MER.	243 of 1897 ...	...	Pāka.

The next sub-division, *sīma* appears but rarely in the Kākatīya inscriptions. Mulkināḍu *sīma* and its sub-division Mukkanṭi *nāḍu* are referred to in an inscription of Cennūr in the Cudappah district dated A. D. 1314 * and Kandukūr *sīma* is mentioned in the last of Pratāparudra's inscriptions which is dated 1329-30. † The earliest record of Vēmaya Reḍḍi dated 1335 also refers to Ammanavabrōli *sīma.* ‡ Therefore, it is certain that '*sīma*' was just coming into use during the latter half of Pratāparudra II's reign.

No administrative division higher than *sīma*, seems to have been known to the Kākatīyas; but Kr. 28 seems to suggest that a higher administrative district was in fact in existence: it mentions the village of 'Arumurigulla included in the *sthala* of Pūnginādu

* *LR.* viii pp. 85-86.

† *NDI.* ii Kr. 28 ; Sewell : *Historical Inscriptions* p. 183.

‡ *MAR.* 1920 : Part i. p. 11.

belonging to Udayagiri in our kingdom,' and speaks of 'the villages of the Kandukūri *sīma*.' It is evident that the highest district was *durga*; and *sīma*, *nādu* and *sthala* came after it. This is not improbable; for the Reḍḍi inscription already mentioned brings to our notice a similar organisation; it refers to the village of Rāma-tīrtham in the Ammanavabrōli *sīma*, in the Śrīśaila *bhūmi*.* The internal organisation of the Kākatīya kingdom is thus seen to be similar to that of Vijaya-nagara. This similarity could not have been the result of accidental development; for the same kind of organisation was also obtaining in the kingdom of Koṇḍavīḍu, which was established by one of the officers of Pratāparudra II, in a part of the Kākatīya dominions. The existence of the same administrative divisions arranged more or less in a similar fashion points to some intimate connection between the king-doms of Warrangal and Vijayanagara which has not yet been recognised. Probably the founders of Vijayanagara, like Prōlaya Vēma Reḍḍi, were also in the service of the Kākatīyas.

One interesting point should be noticed in this connection. *Sthala* and *rājya*, as pointed out already, are occasionally met with in the Hoysala, the Sēuṇa and the Cāḷukya inscriptions; but the term *sīma* is conspicuous by its absence. It makes its appearance for the first time during the last days of the Kākatīyas, and came into universal use under the Reḍḍis and the Rāyas of Vijayanagara. As it was unknown outside the Telugu country in the pre-Vijayanagara days, its presence in the inscriptions of the Canarese districts during the time of the Rāyas shows that it was intro-duced by them when they established their mastery

* *MAR*. 1920 Part i. p. 11.

over the Karṇāṭa country. *Sīma*, therefore, indicates that the organisation of administrative divisions of which it was a part originally came into vogue on the east coast, and it gradually spread westwards with the expansion of the kingdom of Vijayanagara.

Section 3 :—(*b*) The *Nāyakara* System:—The word *nāyakara* or *nāyankara* is familiar to all students of Vijayanagara institutions. It was the name given to the tenure under which the *nāyakas* or the *amara-nāyakas*, as they were sometimes called, held land of the Rāyas. The features of this tenure are made familiar to us by Nuniz who seems to have studied it with some care.

"All the land belongs to the king, and from his hand the captains hold it." * "These nobles are like renters who hold all the land from the king." "They are obliged to maintain six lakhs of soldiers, that is six hundred thousand men and twenty six thousand horses." "They are obliged to maintain" several elephants. In addition to these, "they also pay to him every year sixty lakhs of rents as royal dues." †

The Rāya distributed land among his *nāyakas* so that they might maintain troops for his service. They had to provide him with foot soldiers, horses, and elephants; moreover, they were obliged to pay a tax on their holdings. If they failed to fulfil any one of these conditions, they were severely dealt with, and their estates were confiscated by the government. ‡

This method of distributing land among the *nāyakas* was in practice since the early days of the

* Sewell : *FE.* p. 379.

† *ibid.* p. 373. ‡ *ibid.* p. 389.

First Dynasty. An inscription dated 1339 mentions a certain Poddilapalli Singama Nāyaka who held the village of Dhēnuvakoṇḍa as his *nāykara.* * According to another dated 1352, the son of the *Mahāsāvantādhipati* Balavankada Anki Nāyaka was holding Añjadu-*nāḍu* as his *nāyakara.* † Another dated 1392 refers probably to the *nāyakara* of Tirumalanātha, the grandson of Teppada Nāgaṇṇa. ‡ Another dated 1412 alludes to Sōmagandanahaḷḷi of Hirasu *nāḍu* 'belonging to the office of *nāyaka*' of Hiriya Mudiya Nāyaka. § Another dated 1418 refers to Hammīra *nāḍu* 'belonging to the office of *nāyaka*' of Jāka Mudde Nāyaka. ¶

The *Nāyakara* System has been hitherto regarded as an institution peculiar to the kingdom of Vijayanagara. No trace of *nāyakara* can be discovered in the numerous records of the Hoysalas, the Sēuṇas and the Caḷukyas. A study of the inscriptions of the Kākatīyas brings to light the source from which the Rāyas of Vijayanagara got this system of land tenure. It is stated in an inscription of 1279 that Rudrāmbā granted some place (name effaced) as *nāyankara* to Bolli Nāyaka who was her body-guard. ‖ According to a Gaṇapavaram epigraph dated 1292, Pratāpakumāra Rudradēva Mahārāja granted some place as his *nāyankara* to *Mahāpradhāni* Gangidēva. ** Another

* *NDI.* ii. O. 35.

† *EC.* ix. Dv. 29. ತಮ್ಮ ನಾಯ್ಕರಿಗೆ ಸಲುವ.

‡ *EC.* x. Bg. 15. ತಮಗೆ ಸಲುವ.

§ *EC.* ix An. 44. "ನಮ್ಮ ನಾಯಕ ತನಗೆಸಲುವ."

¶ *EC.* ix An. 4. "ತಮ್ಮ ನಾಯಕ ತನಗೆಸಲುವ."

‖ *SII.* Vol. iv. 705 (*AR.* 254 of 1892).

** *Telingāṇa Inscriptions*: Kākatīya 43.

from Mēḷḷaceruvu dated 1311 mentions the *nāyankara* which Pratāparudradēva Mahārāja granted to a certain Cāmi Yeṟṟāpreggeḍa. * Another inscription of the same date coming from Dāmagallu in the Kurnool district mentions two villages which Pratāparudra granted to a certain Viḍemu Kommarāju as his *nāyakara.* † A Gaṇapēśvaram grant of 1313 alludes to 'Velanāṭi *nāyaka-sthala vṛtti*' which the Kākatīya king gave to his *angarakṣas* Pōlaya Nāyaḍu and Kāli Nāyaḍu. ‡ Lastly, a Penumalli epigraph of 1314 records the grant of twenty-two villages which Pratāparudradēva Mahārāja made to his servant Eṟṟeya, 'the gate-keeper of the royal palace,' for his *nāyankara.* §

The instances mentioned above make it clear that *nāyankara* was an institution which was in existence during the time of the last two Kākatīya rulers. In fact, tradition attributes the introduction of this system to Pratāparudra II. According to the *Pratāpacaritra*, Pratāparudra entrusted the defence of his capital to 77 Velama *nāyakas*, and having divided his kingdom into seventy-seven districts, he distributed them ¶ among the *nāyakas*, so that they might efficiently perform their task. This tradition appears to be based on fact; for the Kaluvacēru grant of Anitalli dated 1423 informs us that Kāpaya Nāyaka, who, subsequent to the death of Pratāparudra, having expelled Muhammadans, became the king of Telingāṇa was served by seventy-five *nāyakas.* ‖ The real author of the reform was probably the queen Rudrāmbā herself. Tradition might have wrongly attributed its origin to

* *ibid.* 50.

† *LR.* xv. p. 287.

‡ *SII.* Vol. iv 952 (*AR.* 135 of 1898).

§ *MER.* 131 of 1917.

¶ *Pratāpacaritra ASPP.* vii. p. 287-8.

‖ *ASPP.* ii. p. 107.

her grandson under whom the *Nāyakara* System came into force.

Whatever might be the manner in which the *Nāyankara* System had arisen, there is no doubt that it came into practice for the first time during the reigns of the last two Kākatīya monarchs. Since the system was unknown in every part of South India and Deccan except in Telingāṇa, the Rāyas of Vijayanagara, must have inherited it from the rulers of that country.

Chapter IV

THE EARLY VIJAYANAGARA KINGS AND THE TELUGU COUNTRY

Section 1:—The foregoing study makes it abundantly clear that the founders of the Vijayanagara kingdom came from the Telugu country included in the erstwhile Kākatīya kingdom. But an objection is urged against the 'Telugu origin', on the ground that both Bukka I and Harihara II are said to have defeated the Āndhras and the Kaḷingas. Since no victory over the Āndhras is mentioned in the inscriptions of Harihara I, it has been suggested that after the death of Harihara, 'the Āndhra country apparently rebelled against Bukka I.' This was the first of a series of rebellions which did not terminate before 1401. "These rebellions of the Telugu country against early Vijayanagara rulers prove that the latter were not acknowledged by the Telugus, a thing which can hardly be believed, if the family of Sangama is supposed to be a Telugu family." *

To meet the objection in a satisfactory manner, it is necessary to discuss the history of the Telugu country after the fall of Warrangal in 1323. Barnī states that the kingdom of Tilang was annexed to the empire of Delhi. "The name of Arangal," he says, "was changed into Sultānpūr, and all the country of Tilang was conquered." Pratāparudra II was taken

* Heras: *The Beginnings*: pp. 118-121. Fr. Heras interprets literally the conventional verses which appear in most of the inscriptions describing the mythical conquests of the donors. This method of interpretation, if followed logically, would lead to absurd conclusions. Scholars who are not familiar with the hyperbolic descriptions indulged in by the authors of the *praśastis* should be cautious, if they want to avoid mistakes, in attempting to interpret them.

prisoner, and despatched to Delhi under the charge of Malik Bedar who had been created Kadar Khān, and Khwāja Hāji, *naib* of *arizi mamālik'*; * but according to Shams-i-Siraj Afif, Pratāparudra, 'the *rāja* of Telingāṇa' 'died on the road' to Delhi. † It would seem, therefore, that the Telugu country was subjugated, and the last of the Kākatīyas died, while being marched to Delhi as a prisoner in 1323. As a matter of fact, however, Pratāparudra seems to have lived probably until 1330; ‡ and the kingdom of the Kākatīyas not only did not perish with the fall of Warrangal, but survived a few years longer, when it appears to have succumbed to the forces of disintegration which usually attacked Indian kingdoms after some great disaster.

The political condition of the Telugu country after the fall of the Kākatīyas is described in an inscription dated 1423 A. D., i.e., exactly a century after the capture of Warrangal by the Mussalmans. Though the information, contained in the record should be considered tradition, its correctness is vouchsafed by contemporary documents. "After Pratāparudra (II) died in freedom, his kingdom was occupied by the Mussalmans. Then Prōlaya Nāyaka rescued the earth from the Muhammadans, just as Varāha rescued it from the waters of the ocean. When Prōlaya became the guest of the *swarga* (i.e., died), Kāpaya Nāyaka, whose valour resembled that of the Sun, assumed control over his kingdom by the command of Viśvēśvara. Then king Kāpaya whose lotus feet were served by seventy-five *nāyakas* protected the earth by the mercy of Viśvēśvara. King Kāpaya not only restored to Brāhmaṇs, the *agrahāras* which were seized by the Muhammadans, but granted them several afresh. When

* *ED.* iii. p. 233. † *ibid.* p. 337. ‡ *NDI.* ii. Kr. 28.

O

Kāpaya went to heaven to serve the feet of Viśvēśvara whom he had already served in various ways on earth, the *nāyakas* retired to their respective places where they began to rule independently." *

The first point that deserves attention in the above passage is the condition of Pratāparudra at the time of his death. It is said that he died 'in freedom', although the evidence of the Muhammadan historians would have us believe that the event took place while he was in captivity. Surprising as the statement is, it does not seem to be altogether void of truth. According to an inscription of Santamagalūru, Pratāparudra was ruling in 1326. † Another inscription dated 1330 registers the grant of land to the temple of Bhramarāmēśvara of Ārumūrugu!!a by the king himself. ‡ These inscriptions make it clear that Pratāparudra was not only alive after 1323, but was ruling his kingdom. How is it possible to reconcile this inference with the explicit statement of Shams-i-Sirāj Afīf that Pratāparudra died in captivity on his way to Delhi? There seems to be but one way out of the difficulty. If it be supposed that an attempt was made by the subjects of the captive king to liberate him from the custody of the officers to whom his safe conduct was entrusted, and that this attempt resulted in a promiscuous fight, during the course of which the prisoner had disappeared, the officers might assume that he died in the fight, and report accordingly to the Sultān. And the historian, Sirāj Afīf who obtained his information from the court, might have incorporated it in his work believing that it was accurate. It is not improbable that what actually had taken place was similar to what has been

* *ASPP.* ii. pp. 93-112.

† *MER.* 308 of 1915. ‡ *NDI.* ii. Kr. 28.

suggested. According to an old tradition, Pratāparudra who was imprisoned by the Mussalmans, was subsequently released. * Singama of the Rēcarla family, one of the officers of Pratāparudra bore the title, *rāyabandīvimōcaka* or the liberator of the king from captivity. † Since this title is mentioned in the inscriptions of the Rēcarla family as early as 1369 it is not unlikely that Singama must have performed some action to deserve it. ‡ As Pratāparudra was made captive only once, it is probable that Singama should have earned the title, by securing his release on the occasion.

Of the successors of Pratāparudra mentioned in the inscription of 1423, not much is known. No doubt the names of Prōlaya and Kāpaya are mentioned in a few epigraphs of the time; § but nothing of importance is recorded about their doings. The period of their rule appears to have been very short, as several independent kingdoms came into being by 1335, or a little later. The most important of them were the kingdoms of (1) Warrangal, (2) Rācakoṇḍa, (3) Koṇḍavīḍu, and (4) Kōrukoṇḍa. As all these states excepting the last came into intimate contact with the kingdom of Vijayanagara, a brief account of each of them may not be out of place.

Section 2:— (1) Warrangal. — Warrangal, and together with it, the province of Telingāṇa properly so called remained in the hands of the Mussalmans until 1344. Sultān Muhammad who visited the place in 1336 made fresh arrangements for the government of the province. He divided Telingāṇa into two districts and appointed separate officers to govern

* cf. *ASPP.* iii pp. 60-61.

† *VV.* Mac. Mss. 14-4-17

‡ *VVC. App.* 4. p. 24.

§ *SII.* iv. 950; *The Sujāta* i. 2.

them.* According to the new arrangement, Nusrat Khān became the ruler of the western district with his capital at Bīdar; and Malik Makbūl or Kābūl took charge of the eastern district, having his headquarters at Warrangal. Sultān Muhammad seems to have shown much wisdom in the choice of the new governors, especially the latter. Malik Makbūl was an Āndhra by birth, and he was known as Kattu before he became a follower of the Prophet. It is said that he was 'a man of high position in his tribe, and he had attracted the favour of the *rāi* of that country.' He was one of those who were taken prisoners to Delhi after the capture of Warrangal. When he reached the metropolis, he presented himself to the Sultān, 'and made his profession of the Muhammadan faith. . . . . The Sultān gave him the name of Makbūl' on conversion, and perceiving 'in him many marks of sagacity and intelligence made him deputy-*Wazir* of Delhi.' † His appointment as the governor of Warrangal was probably due to the Sultān's belief that Malik Makbūl who was a son of the soil would be able to exercise the imperial authority in the conquered province more successfully than a complete stranger. The hopes of the Sultān were not fulfilled; for Makbūl had to face the strong opposition of the Hindu chiefs. One of them whom the Muhammadan historians variously call, Kanya Nāyak, Kanya Pāik, Kabā Nāyand and Kṛṣṇa Nāyak 'gathered strength in the country,' and stirring up a revolt, forced Makbūl, the *naib wazier* to flee to Delhi in or about 1344. ‡

Who was this Kanya Nāyak? § According to Ferishta who refers to him as Kṛṣṇa Nāyak, he was a

* *E.D.* iii. p. 243.

† *ibid.* pp. 367-8.

‡ *ibid.* p. 245.

§ App. C. Note on Kanya Nāyak.

son of Pratāparudra and headed a successful rebellion against the Sultān, and having expelled the governor from Telingāṇa, as noticed already, he established himself at Warrangal. Later on he aided Zafar Khān to overthrow the Sultān's authority at Dēvagiri; but when Zafar became the king of Gulburga under the name of Alā-ud-Din Hasan Gangu Bahmani, the old friendship was forgotten, and Kṛṣṇa Nāyak had to defend himself against Alā-ud-Din's invasions.* Notwithstanding the surrender of some territory to Alā-ud-Din, Kṛṣṇa Nāyak was able to hold his own against the Mussalmans. Therefore, Kṛṣṇa Nāyak played an important part in the history of Telingāṇa about the middle of the fourteenth century. In fact, he re-established the Hindu independence in the country, and maintained it successfully for nearly thirty years in spite of the persistent attacks of the Mussalmans.

Kanya or Kṛṣṇa Nāyak could not have been the king of the Telingās whom Bukka I and Harihara II vanquished. In the first place, Kanya was a relation of their family. Secondly, they would not have been so unwise as to invite the hostility of the king of Telingāṇa who, in virtue of his position in the flank of the Bahmani kingdom, could render to them valuable services, by thwarting Muslim designs upon their territories. As a matter of fact, there seems to have existed some sort of understanding between the royal houses of Warrangal and Vijayanagara. There is reason to believe that the rebellions of Warrangal and Kambīla (the later Vijayanagara) against the Sultān of Delhi were interconnected. The friendship which sprang up at this time was kept up, and whenever the Muhammadans became aggressive, the kings of Warrangal and

* Brigg's *Ferishta*. ii. p. 293.

Vijayanagara combined their forces to check them. Soon after the accession of Muhammad Shah Bahmani I, the Hindu bankers of his kingdom, instigated by the kings of Warrangal and Vijayanagara, melted down the gold coins which he had recently struck. This act so enraged Muhammad Shah that he put to death several of the offenders. Sometime after this, 'the *rājas* of Beejanuggur and Tulingāṇa demanded restitution of the territories wrested from them,' by Alā-ud-Din Hasan Gangu. Muhammad Shah remained silent until he felt strong, and then despatched ambassadors to both the Hindu capitals to demand tribute. "The *rāja* of Tulingāṇa upon this deputed his son Vināyak Dēv with an army to recover Kaulās, while the *rāja* of Beejanuggur sent a considerable force to co-operate." * These events which took place before 1362, show that at the time friendly relations obtained between Warrangal and Vijayanagara, and no war took place between them until then.

Kanya Nāyak suffered heavily in his war with Muhammad Shah. He sustained defeats in several engagements, and had to surrender the district of Gōlkoṇḍa in addition to large sums of money paid as war indemnity and tribute. † His troubles, however, were not at an end; for, the Velamas of Rācakoṇḍa who seem to have entered into an alliance with the Muhammadans most unpatriotically invaded his kingdom at the same time. His affairs seem to have reached a crisis. He was completely exhausted owing to his war with the Mussalmans. His friend, the king of Vijayanagara was not in a position to send him assistance on account of the invasion of his kingdom by the Bahmani Sultān. Therefore, he could offer little

* Brigg's *Ferishta*. ii. p. 301. † *ibid*. ii. pp. 303-7.

or no resistance to the invaders. Anapōta, the chief of Rācakoṇḍa marched into his kingdom, and captured Warrangal, Bhuvanagiri, and Singapura sometime before 1369. * In a battle that was fought at Bhīmavaram he was killed by Māda, the brother of Anapōta. †

Section 3:— (2) Rācakoṇḍa :- The Velamas of the Rēcarla family who were in the service of the Kākatīya kings for generations were in possession of the mountainous tract in the Nalgoṇḍa district of the present Hyderabad state. Their capital Rācakoṇḍa from which the kingdom later derived its name was surrounded by a ring of hills which made its position very nearly impregnable. The exact extent of the territory which was under their control is not yet ascertained. The first historical person of the family is Prasāditya who was a contemporary of Gaṇapati and his daughter Rudrāmbā. ‡ His sons Venna and Sabbi distinguished themselves as great warriors during the reigns of Rudrāmbā, and her successor, Pratāparudra. § Yaṟṟa Dācha, the son of Venna, served in Pratāparudra's campaigns against the Pāṇḍyas. ¶ His eldest son Singama appears to have fought with the Muhammadans, and secured the liberty of Pratāparudra whom they were carrying away as a prisoner to Delhi. Singama seems to have asserted his independence about 1335. Then began a period of bloody feuds and petty warfare among the various nobles of the country; and they went on unchecked for several decades owing to the uninterrupted progress of anarchy. Singama who seems to have been an

* *VVC.* App. 4 .p. 24.

† *VV.* Mac. Mss : 14-4-17. భీమవరమునాఁడ మాదానేన్ని జంపి ఖడ్గధారాయుతు గాయగోవాళ హిందూరాయసురత్రాణ బిరుదము . . . తెచ్చినాఁడు"

‡ *VVC.* pp. 11-12. § *ibid.* pp. 15-16. ¶ *ibid.* pp. 22-23.

aggressive restless sort of person was assassinated by the Kṣatriyas at the fort of Jallipalli which he was besieging; * and he was succeeded by Anapōta, his eldest son. The date of Anapōta's accession to the throne is not known. According to one writer the event took place in 1344. † This date should be considered too early; for Singama, his father is said to have defeated king Kāpaya whose earliest inscription is dated in 1346. ‡ Therefore Anapōta's accession must have taken place a little later.

Anapōta adopted the aggressive policy of his father. He is said to have subdued several forts, and extended the boundaries of his principality. Very soon he came into conflict with two states, Warrangal in the north-east and Koṇḍavīḍu in the south. Although Māda the brother of Anapōta is said to have defeated the Reḍḍis of Koṇḍavīḍu at Dannālakōṭa, he does not seem to have secured any material advantage. § However, his war with Kanya Nāyak of Warrangal was more successful. Anapōta was probably in league with the Bahmani Sultān. He seems to have attacked Kanya while he was engaged in a war with Muhammad Shah Bahmani I, and succeeded sometime before 1369 in capturing Warrangal, Bhuvanagiri, and other places. ¶ It was probably on this occasion that Kanya Nāyak met his death while fighting with Māda, as already mentioned. || Therefore, Anapōta's dominions were considerably extended, as a consequence of this war.

It is said that Anapōta's reign came to an end in 1380; but he seems to have ruled for some more years;

* *VVC.* p. 31.

† Vīrabhadra Row: *HA.* iii. p 20.

‡ *SII.* iv. 950.

§ *VVC.* p. 51.

¶ *Ibid* App. 4.

|| *VV.* Mac. Mss. 14-4-17

for according to the history of the Velugōṭi family, he inflicted a defeat on the armies of the king of Vijayanagara. * Now this event could have taken place only in 1384, when the Vijayanagara king invaded Telingāṇa for the first time. An epigraph belonging to the reign of Harihara II of Vijayanagara dated in that year states that when Bukka II went with the army 'to the Orugal country, the Turukas came and attacked him at Kottakoṇḍa.' † From the association of the Muhammadan attack on Kottakoṇḍa with the despatch of the expedition to Warrangal, it may appear that Warrangal belonged to the Muhammadans; but Warrangal and the surrounding country was not conquered by the Bahmani Sultāns until 1424. ‡ It should have been still in the possession of the Velamas who conquered it about 1369. If Anapōta fought with the armies of Vijayanagara, he could have done so only after 1384. Therefore, his death should have taken place sometime later. The object of the expedition was probably to punish Anapōta for the conquest of the territories of Kanya Nāyak, an ally of the *Rāya* of Vijayanagara. Since the Muhammadans attempted to prevent the army from reaching Warrangal, it is reasonable to believe that there existed at the time some sort of alliance between the Rācakoṇḍa chiefs and the Sultāns of Gulburga. Nevertheless, Bukka seems to have won a victory over the Velama chiefs; for Lakṣmaṇācārya, the

* "దరిని దద్భుకర కరవాల హాళికిని కర్ణాటసేనలు గకవలించు." *VVC.* p. 40.

† *EC.* xii. Ck. 15. This place is in the N. W. of Warrangal. (Sewell: *Historical Inscriptions* p. 203).

‡ Ferishta ii. p. 406. Sewell is of opinion that this event took place in 1364, 'when the Bahmani forces finally destroyed the Kākatīya kingdom of Warrangal.' *Historical Inscriptions* p. 203. But this opinion is contradicted by Ferishta and the inscriptions

prāṇācārya of Bukka states in his *Vaidyarājavallabha* that his patron 'conquered the Āndhra kings.' *

The kingdom of Rācakoṇḍa was divided into two halves during the reign of Anapōta. One half with the capital Rācakoṇḍa was directly under Anapōta's rule; and another with the important fort of Dēvarakoṇḍa was governed by Māda, his younger brother. † Anapōta was succeeded at Rācakoṇḍa by his son Singama II who became famous as an author and patron of men of letters. ‡ Māda was succeeded by his son Pedda Vêdagiri. § It was during the time of this prince that the Vijayanagara army invaded Telingāṇa for the second time. The expedition was commanded by one of Harihara's capable officers called Guṇḍa or Guṇḍa Daṇḍanātha. It is stated in an epigraph of Yaṛraguḍi-dinne in the Kurnool district dated 1370 A. D. that Guṇḍa was the son of a certain Salakaladēva, and that he was the lord of Alampura. ¶ According to another inscription in the Kēśavaswāmi temple at Bēlūr, Guṇḍa conquered Āndhra in addition to several other countries enumerated therein. ‖ In his Āndhra campaigns, he seems to have been greatly helped by a certain Gonka Raḍḍi Nāyaka; and in recognition of his services Guṇḍa secured for Gonka the governorship of Mullanāḍu in Coorg. ** Although Guṇḍa claims victory over the Āndhras, Pedda Vēdagiri seems to have defeated and driven him back. The date of this expedition is not ascertained yet. As the inscription of Gonka Raḍḍi is dated in 1390, Guṇḍa's expedition against the Āndhras may be assigned to an earlier date.

* *MAR.* 1919 p. 53.

† *VVC.* p. 33.

‡ *ibid.* p. 59.

§ *ibid* p. 51 ff.

¶ *LR.* 40 p. 209.

‖ *EC.* v. Bl. 3.

** *ibid.* i. Cg. 39.

The hostility between the rulers of Vijayanagara and Rācakoṇḍa continued for another quarter of a century or more until Dēvarāya I by following a policy of conciliation won the permanent friendship of the Velamas. The history of the relations between Rācakoṇḍa and Vijayanagara subsequent to the death of Harihara II does not concern us here as they fall outside the period of our enquiry.

Section 4:—(3) Koṇḍavīḍu: Prōlaya Vēma, the founder of the Reḍḍi kingdom of Koṇḍavīḍu was an officer under Pratāparudra II. On the death of his master, he attempted to seize the Telugu country south of the Kṛṣṇa; but was only partly successful, as he was able to establish his authority over a limited area only, extending from the river Kṛṣṇa to Kandukūr in the north of the Nellore district and from the Bay of Bengal to the Śrīśaila mountain in the Kurnool district. Large portions of Nellore, Kurnool, Anantapūr, and Beḷḷāry districts and the whole of Cuddapah over which Pratāparudra ruled appear to have slipped out of his hands, on account of circumstances which have not yet come under our purview. If after the death of Pratāparudra anarchy were prevailing here, as in the other parts of the kingdom, Prōlaya Vēma would not have found it difficult to subjugate this region also. His failure to bring under his sway the whole of the southern Telugu country, especially Nellore which was the birth-place of his family, * points to the existence of some obstacle which he could not overcome. Some

* The following passage of Śrīnātha describes the quarter in which the Reḍḍis of Koṇḍavīḍu originally rose to prominence.

"చతుర్థకులమౌళి మండనంబై కీర్తివిహార ఘంటాపథంబైన పంటమహాన్వయంబు పాకనాటిదేశంబున భద్రపీఠంబు నధివసించి సింహవిక్రమనగర దువ్వూరు గండవరాలిపట్టణంబులు నిజనివాసంబులుగా భూతలాదష్టాష్టాదశద్వీపాంతరాళంబుల

ten years later, this area was included in the dominions of the *Rāyas* of Vijayanagara. It is not unreasonable to suppose that they were in possession of it from the time of Pratāparudra. This, however, is a mere suggestion, and it may be taken for what it is worth.

Whatever be the causes which prevented Prōlaya Vēma from imposing his yoke over the whole of the southern Telugu country, he managed to hold what he seized until 1350. According to one writer, he declared his independence at Vinukoṇḍa about 1328.* As he pushed his conquests eastwards, he appears to have found it to be unsuitable as his capital; therefore, he shifted the head-quarters of his government to Addanki, at present a village in the Ongōle tālūka of the Guntūr district.

Prōlaya Vēma could not have been very friendly with the *Rāyas* of Vijayanagara. He wanted to acquire as much territory as he could conquer in the southern Telugu country; and the *Rāyas* seem to have felt an irresistible attraction towards the Kṛṣṇa. Although no outbreak of war between the two states is recorded, Prōlaya Vēma seems to have sustained some loss of territory. The district of Vinukoṇḍa belonged, as already noticed, to him from the day on which he laid the foundations of his new kingdom; but it passed into the hands of Bukka I sometime before 1352.† This transference of territory could not have been effected by peaceful means.

భూపాలగ్రామణులం త్రిలింగ భూమండలాఖండలురను బ్రోలయ వేమన్న
పోతాన్న వేము కుమార గిరీశ్వరాములం బూజ్యసామ్రాజ్యపీఠస్థులం గాంచె."

Bhimēśvarapurāṇam 1 : 31.

* Vīrēśalingam Pantulu : *The Lives of Poets* p. 66. (1911 Edition).

† *VR.* iii. Kl. 56, 58.

Prōlaya Vēma was succeeded by his eldest son, Anapōta. He ruled for a period of twelve years from 1350 to 1362. His reign was on the whole prosperous, notwithstanding his frequent wars with the Velamas of Rācakoṇḍa. For some reason, unknown at present, he was obliged to change the head-quarters of his government. The capital of the kingdom was at first Addanki in the Ongōle tālūka of the Gunṭūr district. Anapōta abandoned this city, and repaired to the wild hilly tract in the north-east of Palnāḍ, where he built a fort on the top of a rock. * This was the famous fort of Koṇḍavīḍu which was destined to play an important part in the history of the east-coast during the next two or three centuries. The change of the capital was probably due to the ever-increasing pressure of the governors of Udayagiri upon his southern frontier. Anapōta died in 1362 and was succeeded by his younger brother Anavēma. During his reign, there appears to have been some trouble in the northern districts of the kingdom. The country between the rivers Kṛṣṇa and Gōdāvari was included in the Reḍḍi kingdom since the days of his father; there seems to have been a rebellion in this region; for according to one of his inscriptions at Śrīśailam, Anavēma destroyed Rājamahēndrapura, Niravadyapura and other *sthala-durgas.* Having ruled for a period of nineteen years, Anavēma died in A. D. 1381, and was succeeded by his nephew Kumāragiri. The decline of the Reḍḍi kingdom began with the accession of Kumāragiri. He was a lover of ease and pleasure. In spite of the efforts of Kāṭaya-Vēma, his brother-in-law and minister, he

* *Elliot Collection*: p. 270; Prabhākara Śāstri: *Śṛngāra Śrīnātham*. p. 52.

Tatōnnapōta nṛpatiḥ paṭuḥ pālana karmaṇi
Apālayat tasya putraḥ tamdamtē'ndhra vasundharām ‖
Koṇḍavīḍum rājadhānim savicitrām akalpayat
Dṛṣṭvā tvaṣṭāpi vaicitryaṁ abhūdyasyāḥ savismayaḥ ‖

lost a good deal of territory within four or five years of his accession. Harihara II conquered the regions surrounding Śrīśailam and Tripurāntakam before 1386; and his son Dēvarāya who became the governor of Udayagiri about 1380, captured the old Reḍḍi capital, and annexed the territory along the east-coast extending as far as Mōṭupalli before A. D. 1390. * As a consequence of these aggressions, Kumāragiri Reḍḍi lost nearly one third of his dominions; but he managed to keep his authority over the rest until 1403 A. D., when he seems to have died.

The internal affairs of the kingdom of Vijayanagara soon offered an opportunity for the ruler of Koṇḍavīḍu to recover what he had lost. During the last years of Harihara II, there seems to have been much uncertainty about the succession to the throne. Harihara II had several sons whom he employed as the governors of provinces. Three of them, princes Dēvarāya, Immaḍi Bukka, and Virūpaṇṇa rose to prominence, and each of them entertained hopes of ascending the throne. Dēvarāya or Prauḍha Dēvarāya, as he is sometimes called, was the crown prince and he was the governor of the important fortress of Udayagiri from 1382 onwards. Immaḍi Bukka was a famous warrior, and he was governing the province of Mulbāgal about 1391. Virūpaṇṇa was the governor of the Tamil country from 1380 onwards and he succeeded to the power and influence of Kampaṇa II.

* The last Reḍḍi inscriptions at Tripurāntakam and Śrīśailam are dated in A. D. 1356, and 1377 respectively. (*MER*. 185 of 1905; 20 of 1915). The earliest of the Vijayanagara inscriptions at Tripurāntakam is dated in 1386 (*MER*. 257 of 1905); and although the earliest Vijayanagara record at Śrīśailam is dated in A. D. 1393 (*MER*. 49 of 1915), it would have been impossible for the Reḍḍis to maintain their authority here after they lost their hold on Tripurāntakam. Dēvarāya's conquest of Addanki is indicated in one of his copper-plate grants; (*NDI*. i. Cp. I); and his control over the east-coast as far as Mōṭupalli is shown by the charter which he granted to the merchants of that sea-port town. (*LR*. 42. pp. 422-23).

According to an old record, Harihara II seems to have fallen ill sometime before 1404. * On hearing the news of his illness, all his three sons mentioned above, hastened to Vijayanagara, so that they might watch their respective interests personally. † Harihara II died in 1404; ‡ and his death seems to have been followed by the outbreak of a civil war which disturbed the peace of the kingdom during the next two years. §

The internal disturbances did not fail to attract the attention of the enemies of Vijayanagara. Feroz Shah, the Sultān of Gulburga, invaded the Rāicūr doab ¶ and the Reḍḍis, taking advantage of the absence of the army from Udayagiri, invaded that province in 1406 and occupied it for sometime. The Reḍḍi forces which were commanded by Cennā Reḍḍi-Annā Reḍḍi-Mallā Reḍḍi subdued the districts of Pottapi and Pulugula nāḍu. || They thus had the satisfaction of turning the tables over their enemies. The expulsion of the Reḍḍis and the reconquest of Udayagiri by Dēvarāya I are subjects that do not come under the scope of the present discussion.

What has been said so far is enough to establish the identity of the Āndhra enemies of Bukka I and Harihara II. They were the Velamas of Rācakoṇḍa,

* *LR.* 22. p. 166. † *ibid.* 22. p. 166. cf. *LR.* 17. p. 178.

‡ *EC.* viii. Tl. 129.

§ Harihara's successor Dēvarāya I did not ascend the throne until Śaka 1329 *Sarvajit*, *Kārttika ba* 10 Thursday (*LR* 13. p. 257, Mārkāpuram). In an inscription of A. D. 1406, it is said that he was permanently placed on the throne (*EC.* x. Pg. 33). In another (*EC.* x. Mb. 175) he is said to have been permanently anointed to the throne of Vijayanagara.

¶ Sewell : *The Forgotten Empire* p. 50.

|| *LR.* 22. p. 166. (Inscription at Tangaṭūr in the Cudappah Dt.) ; *MER.* 433 of 1911.

and the Reḍḍis of Koṇḍavīḍu. The former, it should be noted, had the title of *Āndhra-dēśādhīśvara.* * Bukka I and his son waged wars on them not to suppress any rebellion, but to destroy their independence by conquering their respective kingdoms. The Telugu people of the southern and the western districts never rose up in rebellion against them but remained submissive to them and their descendants. Therefore, the subjugation of the Āndhras mentioned in the inscriptions of Bukka I and Harihara II cannot at all be said to be incompatible with their Telugu origin, as the conquered Telugu country belonged to the kingdoms of Rācakoṇḍa and Koṇḍavīḍu.

* *VVC.* App. Inscription 5 p. 26. స్వస్తి శ్రీవిజయాభ్యుదయ శకవర్షంబులు ౧౩౦౨ అగు రౌద్రి సంవత్సర శ్రావణ శుద్ధ ౯ స్వస్తి శ్రీమన్మహామండలేశ్వర ఆంధ్రదేశాధీశ్వర . . . . వీరశ్రీరాయ రావు అన పోతనాయనింగారు.

CHAPTER V.

THE EXPANSION OF THE KINGDOM OF VIJAYANAGARA.

Section 1:—The tract of territory over which Vīra Kampiladēva ruled should be regarded as the nucleus around which the empire of Vijayanagara had grown up; for it was entrusted to Harihara I by Sultān Muhammad a few years after he had overthrown Kampila. The date on which Sultān Muhammad appointed Harihara as the governor of the conquered country is not known. In the light of the information supplied by the Muhammadan historians, it can only be said that Harihara was appointed sometime between 1327 and 1344. However, a study of Harihara's inscriptions may enable us to ascertain the date more precisely. According to the Kāpalūr plates, he was reigning at Kuñjarakōna in 1336. * As this grant is declared spurious, the date it supplies may not be considered trustworthy; but it is not improbable that Harihara should have been ruling the country then; for according to the Aṭakalaguṇḍa † and the Bādāmi ‡ inscriptions dated 1339-40, he was the lord of extensive territories which he had conquered extending from the eastern to the western sea. It would have taken at least some two or three years to effect the conquest of the land lying between the Bay of Bengal and the Arabian Sea. In that case, he should have been ruling the kingdom of Kampila either from 1336 or the next year. That coincides roughly with the date supplied by the Kāpalūr and the Yeṟṟaguḍi plates. § Therefore,

* *NDI*. Cp. 15.

† *LR*. 23 pp. 52-53.

‡ *IA*. x. p. 63.

§ *EC*. x. Bg. 70.

it may be assumed, at the present state of our knowledge, that Harihara's appointment should have taken place in A. D. 1336 or even a little earlier.

The exact extent of territory which the Sultān entrusted to his care is not known; but it may be safely assumed that it included almost the whole of the present Beḷḷāry district, and a portion of the doab between the Tungabhadra and the Kṛṣṇa. A close scrutiny of Harihara's inscriptions shows that he rapidly extended his dominions by conquering the lands of his neighbours, and that the process of conquest gradually spread from the east to the west. It is stated in an inscription at Śṛngēri * dated 1346 that Harihara had conquered 'the earth from the eastern to the western ocean.' Mārapa 'acquired a kingdom in the west' from Kallasa. † This conquest of 'the earth from the eastern to the western ocean' should have been completed before 1339-40; for in the Aṭakalaguṇḍa and the Bādāmi inscriptions referred to above, Harihara assumes the significant title of '*Pūrva-Paścima-Samudrādhipati*,' or 'the lord of the eastern and the western ocean'. As the kings of Vijayanagara never maintained a fleet to control the seas, the expression should be taken to mean the sovereignty of the land bordering on both the seas. As a matter of fact, Harihara I was ruling on both the coasts about 1340. According to a Koḍavalūru epigraph, Kampaṇa I was ruling in the Nellore district in 1347. ‡ Another epigraph near the Buggabhāvi at Udayagiri dated 1343, records a gift of Kampaṇa to a deity. § Therefore, Kampaṇa's rule over Udayagiri should have begun either in 1342 or a little earlier. Now, Bukka I had a son of the name of Virūpaṇṇa. ¶

* *EC.* vi. Sg. 1.

† *EC.* viii. Sb. 375.

‡ *NDI.* ii. Nr. 28.

§ *LR.* 46. pp. 236-37.

¶ *EC.* viii. Tl. 16, 28, 37, 125.

The term 'Uddagiri' is frequently prefixed to his name in his inscriptions. 'Uddagiri' is the contracted form of Udayagiri. In order to acquire the epithet 'Uddagiri,' he must have been either born in the place, or should have been its governor for sometime. If he was born at Udayagiri, when could the event have happened? Virūpaṇṇa was posted in 1344 to Penugoṇḍa * which Harihara I or his brother Bukka conquered from the Hoysalas between 1340 and 1344. They would not have placed a conquered district under the charge of an infant. If it be assumed that Virūpaṇṇa was at least ten years old at the time of his appointment as the commandant of the fortress of Penugoṇḍa, he should have been born about 1334 ; and if his birth took place at Udayagiri, that fort should have been in the possession of his father at the time. If, on the other hand, the other alternative is accepted, Virūpaṇṇa should have been the governor of Udayagiri before 1343 ; for the family of Kampaṇa I who began to rule the district in that year continued to hold it until 1380 or even later. In order that the name Udayagiri should become specially associated with Virūpaṇṇa, he ought to have been connected with the administration of the province for a comparatively long period of time. In any case, the Nellore district in which Udayagiri is situated, seems to have 'formed a portion of the original Vijayanagara kingdom.' †

Section 2 :— The conquest of the west coast was also effected more or less at the same time. It is evident from the statement of Ibn Battūta that Konkan acknowledged the supremacy of Vijayanagara in 1342. ‡ The conquest of the country should have taken

* Sewell : *L.A.* i. p. 119-20. Penugoṇḍa 23.

† *NDI.* iii. p. 1468.

‡ Ibn Battūta : *Travels* : (Broadway Travellers) : p. 230.

place before that date. Harihara I is said to have constructed a fort at Bārakūru in 1336 A. D. * As this statement is based on tradition whose authenticity cannot be proved, it may be set aside as unreliable. There can be little doubt that Harihara invaded South Canara in 1338. A Hoysala epigraph dated in that year records a visit of Ballāḷa III to his army stationed at Bārakūru. † He commanded Ankeya Nāyaka, his general in charge of the army 'to remain in Bārakūru.' When Ankeya replied, "I will stay, *Jiya*," Ballāḷa was so pleased with the answer that he granted him the village of Aladahaḷḷi. It is evident that Bārakūru was attacked by some enemy in 1338, whom the Hoysala generals were not able to check. Their position appears to have become precarious and Ballāḷa entertained serious doubts about the safety of Bārakūru, the capital of the district. Therefore, he personally visited the place to encourage his army. When the officer Ankeya said that he would stay at the post of duty, Ballāḷa was so pleased that he rewarded him with the grant of a village. This probably indicates the desperate character of the work which the officer had undertaken to do in the face of danger. Who was the enemy that attacked the Hoysalas in this part of their kingdom ? It is asserted that the Āḷupas attacked the Hoysala generals at Bārakūru and that Ballāḷa went to the place to defend it. "The rulers of Tuluva were the Āḷupas, and their capital was Bārakūru. It was to break the power of the Āḷupas that the Hoysala ruler visited the Tuluva centre." ‡ This, however, is not possible. Although the conquest of the Tuḷuva country was undertaken by Ballāḷa III as early as 1319, it could not have been completed before 1333 ; for, none

* Sturrock : *South Canara Manual.* i. p. 55.

† *EC.* v. Ak. 183.

‡ *Jr. Bom. Hist. Soc.* ii. p. 121.

of his inscriptions bearing an earlier date is found in South Canara, though several of a later date have been noticed all over the district.

Reference.	Date.	Place.	Contents.
M. E. R :— 492 of 1928-29	1333	Nilavara, Uḍipi Tālūka.	14 members of the assembly of the village of Niruvara made a gift of taxes on lands to Durgā Bhagavatī in the presence of the queen Cikkāyi Tāyigaḷu with the permission of Vaicappa Daṇṇāyaka and other officers.
493 of 1928-29	1334	do.	Mentions the chief queen Bukkāyi Tāyigaḷu and the village of Niruvara.
583 of 1930.	1336	Bailūr, Uḍipi Tālūka.	Records the grant of *samudāya* tax accruing from the village of Bayilūru by the queen Kikkāyi Tāyi to a certain Vasudēva Mudaliar; and mentions *Mahāpradhāna* Baicappa Nāyaka and *Nakhara Hanjumanas* of Bārakūru.
122 of 1901.	1336	Mudakēri near Bārakūru.	Mentions Vaicappa Daṇṇāyaka and *Mahāpradhāna* Ajjaṇa Śāhiṇi.

Reference.	Date.	Place.	Contents.
M. E. R :— 566 of 1930.	1338	Hatyan-gadi, Coondā-poor Tālūka.	Mentions Kōṭiśvara.
43 of 1901.	1341	Gurugala basti, Mudabi-dure.	Mentions Dēvappa Daṇṇāyaka.

The authority of Ballāḷa, as shown by this schedule, was recognised until 1341. There is no indication of an Āḷupa rebellion during this period. On the contrary, the Āḷupas seem to have remained submissive under his rule. If, under the circumstances, Bārakūru was threatened by an enemy, that enemy should have come from outside. The only foe who could have attempted the conquest of this region was Harihara; therefore, it must have been his invasion of Bārakūru which compelled Ballāḷa III to go to the front. It is interesting to note that the queen Kikkāyi Tāyi, mentioned in these inscriptions, played an important part in the administration of the Tuḷu country during the reigns of both Ballāḷa III and Harihara I. Who was she? and what was her place in the administrative machinery of the province? It is suggested that she was the queen of Ballāḷa III.* This is not improbable. She was, however, an Āḷupa by birth. The titles *Pāṇḍyacakravarti*, *Basavaśankara*, *and* *Rāyagajāṅkuśa* which she bore establish her kinship with the Āḷupa

* *MER.* 1928-9. Part ii. p. 81.

rulers of Bārakūru. * Ballāḷa III might have married her for political reasons on his conquest of the territory of the Āḷupas. It is interesting to note that this queen survived Ballāḷa and became a subordinate of Harihara I. She was one of Harihara's subordinates who attended in 1346 the festival which he celebrated at Sṛngēri in honour of his conquest of the earth from 'the eastern to the western ocean.' On this occasion she granted to Bhāratī Tīrtha Śrīpāda the village of Hosavūr in Santalige nāḍu for the maintenance of his servants. † Kikkāyi Tāyi who was the queen of Ballāḷa III would not have become a subordinate of the king of Vijayanagara without a struggle. It is obvious that the Tuḷu country was conquered by Harihara I. Although the Hoysalas ruled in parts of South Canara until 1341, it is not improbable that Harihara's invasion should have taken place three years earlier.

Section 3 :—The conquest of the Hoysala Kingdom.—In the opinion of some writers, the founders of Vijayanagara did not acquire the Hoysala dominions by conquest, but obtained them as a legacy from a grateful monarch for meritorious services rendered on the field of battle. ‡ "Even the feudatory petty kings who served under the Hoysalas at once transferred their allegiance to Harihara." § This is far from the truth. Harihara I and his brothers had, in fact, to wage several wars with the Hoysala monarchs and their dependents before they could establish their authority over the Hoysala territories.

When exactly the struggle between the Hoysalas and the founders of Vijayanagara began, it is not known. By 1338, as pointed out already, war had

* *EC.* vi. Sg. 1 ; *MAR.* 1916. p. 57. † *ibid.*

‡ Heras: *The Beginnings* p. 106. § *ibid.* p. 127.

broken out between them in Konkan. At the same time, hostilities seem to have commenced in the Kōlār district on the eastern frontier of the Hoysala kingdom. Ballāḷa III seems to have entrusted its defence to Ballappa Daṇṇāyaka, the younger brother of Ḍāti Singeya Daṇṇāyaka. A few inscriptions bearing dates from 1337 to 1339 record the grants of some private individuals 'for the success of the sword and arm of Ballappa Daṇṇāyaka.'

Reference.	Date.	Donor.	Object.
EC. x. Ci. 53	1337	The great Pāśāyita Daṇṇāyakar, and the inhabitants of Periyanāḍu	"For the victory to the arm of the great minister Dādi Singeya Nāyakar's younger brother Ballappa Daṇṇāyakar."
EC. x. Kl. 54	1339	Dēvappar of Koḍambuḷiyūr.	"For the success of the sword and arm of Śrī Pōśana Vīra Vallāla's son Periya Vallappa Daṇṇāyakar."
EC. x. Bp. 28	1339	Four subordinates of Ballappa Daṇṇāyaka.	"For the success of the sword and arm of Dāti Singeya Nāyaka's younger brother Ballappa Daṇṇāyakar."

Ballappa Daṇṇāyaka was evidently fighting during these years with some enemy who attacked the Hoysala kingdom from the east. Who could have been the enemy against whom he was fighting ? It has been suggested that the fighting recorded in these inscriptions took place in the Nigarili Śōḷamaṇḍalam, a district included in the Cōḷamaṇḍala. Therefore, these inscriptions are said to 'refer to a war against the Muhammadans of the south.' * Nigarili Śōḷamaṇḍalam where the fighting was going on during these years, was not in Cōḷamaṇḍala. It was the name by which the present Kōlār district was known during the Hoysala times. The name was originally given to it by the Cōḷas in the tenth or the early eleventh century, † and the Hoysala monarchs who succeeded them in this part of their empire preserved the Cōḷa administrative system intact. Consequently the names which the Cōḷas gave to the administrative divisions survived their empire and it was how the Kōlār district came to be known as Nigarili Śōḷamaṇḍalam during the rule of the Hoysala monarchs. It is inconceivable how the Muhammadans of the south *i. e.*, of Madura could have come so far north as the Kōlār district and offered battle to Ballappa Daṇṇāyaka. If Ballappa fought in Kōlār against the Muhammadans of Madura in 1337, his adversary should have been Sheriff Jalāl-ud-Din Ahsan Shah, the founder of the Madura sultanate. Ibn Battūta, a son-in-law of Jalāl-ud-Din who paid a visit to Madura in 1343 gives an account of the history of the sultanate of Madura.

"Formerly, the country of Ma'bar had submitted to the authority of Sultān Muhammad of Dihly (Delhi). A revolt was stirred up amongst his followers by my father-in-law, the Sheriff Djelaleddin Ahsan Shah (Sheriff Jalāl-ud-Din Ahsan Shah) who reigned there for five years, after which he was killed and replaced by one of his *amīrs*, Alauddin Odeidjy (Alā-ud-Din Uḍauji) who governed for one year. At the end of this

* *Jr. Bom. Hist. Soc.* ii p. 121. † *EC.* x. Intr. p. 24.

time he set out to conquer the infidels; he took a considerable amount of riches and ample spoils from them and returned to his own state. The following year he led a second expedition against the idolators and routed them and massacred a large number. The same day on which he inflicted this disaster upon them it happened that he took off his helmet in order to drink; an arrow shot by an unknown hand struck him and he died on the field. His son-in-law, Kotbeddin (Qutb-ud-Din) Feroz was placed upon the throne; but as his conduct was generally disapproved of, he was killed at the end of forty days. The Sultān Ghiyatheddin (Ghiyās-ud-Din) was invested with authority, he married the daughter of the Sultān and Sheriff Djelaleddin. It is the sister of this same girl that I had married at Dihly (Delhi)." *

The rebellion of Sheriff Jalāl-ud-Din broke out in 1335. † In order to suppress this rebellion, Sultān Muhammad marched at the head of an army to Ma'bar. When he reached Warrangal in 1336, he was stricken with disease, so that he had to abandon the idea of going to Ma'bar at the time. ‡ The troubles of the Sultān which prevented him in the succeeding years to resume the campaign could not have been known to Jalāl-ud-Din in 1337. Therefore, he should have been expecting the arrival of the Delhi army at any time. Moreover, Ibn Battūta does not refer to any campaign of his father-in-law against the infidels, although he takes particular care to record all the expeditions of Alā-ud-Din Uḍauji and Ghiyās-ud-Din. It is unlikely that Sheriff Jalāl-ud-Din should have undertaken an expedition against the kingdom of Ballāḷa III in the year

* *South Ind. Mah. In.* App. B. p. 235.

† *ibid.* p. 154.

‡ Barnī: *ED.* iii, p. 243.

succeeding his rebellion. In fact the Muhammadans of the south did not come into conflict with Ballāḷa until 1340. By that time Jalāl-ud-Din was assassinated and Alā-ud-Din Uḍauji ascended the throne.

The enemy who attacked the eastern frontier of the Hoysalas in 1337 should have been the master of the adjacent Telugu country. The northern part of the Anantapūr district passed into the hands of Harihara I before 1340. The fort of Gutti has been described in an undated epigraph as "the navel to the wheel of sovereignty over the whole earth of the illustrious king Bukka." * It is also said that it increased his fortune. This refers to a period when Gutti was the centre of the territory over which Bukka I ruled. After 1340, Bukka began his conquest of the Hoysala dominions from the east. Very soon he shifted the head-quarters of his government to Hosapaṭṭaṇa in the Hoysāṇa country. No doubt, he had an alternate capital in the Anantapūr district, but that was no longer Gutti but Penugoṇḍa. † Therefore the Gutti inscription should be assigned to a date earlier than 1340. This is corroborated by the Aṭakala-guṇḍa epigraph of Harihara I dated 1339 in which he is said to have been ruling the earth with Gutti as his *nelevīḍu.* ‡ It follows from this that he was the master of the Telugu country to the east of the Hoysala kingdom. Ballappa Daṇṇāyaka should have been fighting not against the Muhammadans of the south, but against Bukka I, the most prominent of the five brothers who founded the kingdom of Vijayanagara.

The conquest of the Hoysala kingdom properly so called may be said to have begun in 1341. Ballāḷa III was summoned to his southern frontier to defend it

* *SII.* i. p. 167. † *MER.* 522 of 1906. ‡ *LR.* 23. pp 52-53.

against the inroads of Alā-ud-Din Uḍauji, the Sultān of Madura. Before he left his capital, Ballāḷa III is said to have performed the *abhiṣēka* of his son Vīra Ballāḷa Rāya * so that in the northern part of the kingdom, people might not feel the absence of their sovereign, and forget the obligations of loyalty. Probably, he had also some sort of presentiment of the disaster which was to overtake him ere long on the battle-field of Beribi or Trichinopoly. Having entrusted the kingdom to the care of a new monarch, and a faithful body of ministers, he took his departure from Dōrasamudra never more to return.

In the meanwhile, Sultān Uḍauji whose military activities summoned Ballāḷa III to the south was assassinated by an unknown enemy; and he was ultimately succeeded by Ghiyās-ud-Din who turned out to be more inhuman than his predecessor. It was against this ruler that Ballāḷa III marched at the head of his army which 'exceeded hundred thousand men.' In addition to these, Ballāḷa had in his service 'twenty thousand Mussalmans.' No information is available regarding the operations during the first year of the war; but it is certain that nothing serious happened. At the beginning of the next year, a battle was fought at a place called Cobban, and the Muhammadans met with a crushing disaster. They fled in confusion to Madura, their capital, leaving the garrison at Cobban to defend itself as well as it could. † The

* *EC.* ix. Bn. 111. It is extremely doubtful whether this inscription refers to the coronation of the son of Ballāḷa. It records a gift of *Naralōkagaṇḍa* Mayileya Nāyaka's brother Cenneya Nāyaka for the perpetuation of the reign of his nephew, Mayileya Nāyaka-Cenneya Nāyaka. The expression "*rājyābhiṣēkamāḍalāgi*" does not seem to have any connection with what follows it; and the expression '*dēvara kumāra*' qualifies *Mahāsāmantādhipati Naralōkagaṇḍa* Kōḍiya Nāyaka.

† *South. Ind. Muh. In.* App. B. p. 238.

defeat of the Muhammadan army left the path to the interior of the Madura kingdom open ; and Ballāḷa marched triumphantly as far as Rāmēśvaraṃ where he set up a pillar of victory. * Having thus demonstrated his strength, he returned to Cobban where he busied himself in attempting to take the place.

The handful of Muhammadans who defended Cobban against Ballāḷa were hard pressed. Their supplies were very nearly exhausted. Ballāḷa who had no desire to kill them offered them safe conduct, if they would abandon the fort and retire. They replied that they could not do anything without consulting their Sultān. Ballāḷa thereupon declared a truce of fourteen days during which the Muhammadan soldiers were expected to communicate with their Sultān, and obtain his opinion. When the news of the sad condition of the garrison at Cobban reached Madura, the Sultān collected a body of 3,000 soldiers and approached Cobban by rapid marches. Ballāḷa was off his guard, probably under the notion that the enemy would not attack him so long as the truce lasted; but the Muhammadans who were at Cobban had no respect for conventions. They suddenly fell upon the Hindu host during the hour of *siesta.* Ghiyās-ud-Din with his troops appeared on the scene in time to complete the discomfiture of the Hindus. All was confusion and disorder in the Hindu camp and they were easily defeated. Ballāḷa III himself fell into the hands of his enemies. At first, he was imprisoned and treated with consideration. When the Sultān extorted from him as much money as he could, he had him murdered in his prison. †

* *EC.* xi. Mr. 32.

† *South Ind. Muh. In.* App. B. 239. Ballāḷa was killed, according to an inscription (*EC.* iv. Kd. 75), on the battle field of Beribi on Sept. 8, 1342; but

The long absence of Ballāḷa in the south, his subsequent defeat at the hands of the Mussalmans and ultimate death in prison seem to have let loose the forces of disintegration which soon undermined the foundations of the Hoysala kingdom. Ballāḷa IV was solemnly crowned at Dōrasamudra in 1343; * but he appears to have made no effort to restore the fast disappearing fortunes of his family. Under the circumstances, the Hoysala kingdom should have appeared a very tempting morsel for invaders to grab at; and they soon made their appearance on the scene.

Harihara I and his brothers had already made themselves masters of bits of Hoysala territory here and there. They now proceeded to subjugate the whole kingdom in a systematic fashion. While Ballāḷa IV was being crowned at Dōrasamudra, their

Ibn Battūta declares that he was taken prisoner. Sultān Ghiyās-ud-Din, having extorted from Ballāḷa all his wealth, 'had him killed and flayed; his skin was stuffed with straw, and hung upon the wall of Moutra (Madura), where I saw it suspended.' (*South Ind. Muh. In.* App. B. p. 239). Since Battūta saw the stuffed skin of Ballāḷa hanging on the walls of Madura, it is clear that he did not die on the battle field. This view is also indirectly supported by the evidence of the inscriptions. Ballāḷa III, as mentioned already, is said to have died on 8th Sept. 1342. His son's coronation did not take place until June 28, 1343. There was thus an interval of nearly ten months between the supposed date of Ballāḷa III's death and the coronation of his son. The reason for this long interval is not clear, unless we suppose that Ballāḷa was in the hands of the enemy who was holding out hopes of release until he extorted all his wealth from him. If Ghiyās-ud-Din succeeded in squeezing his wealth from Ballāḷa, he should have allowed the prisoner to communicate with his officers, so that they might furnish him the necessary ransom. In that case, the fact that he was alive after the battle would be known to his officers, and also to his son. So long as Ballāḷa was alive, there was no need for the celebration of his son's coronation. When, however, the news of his murder reached Dōrasamudra, the coronation was celebrated. The wrong date given in Kd. 75 can only be explained in one way. It is a *viragal* inscription set up in memory of a common soldier who died fighting at Beribi, by a relation living in a remote part of the country. Again the memorial stone was set up 22 years after the death of the soldier. The author of the *viragal* inscription should have incorporated the general belief in the country that Ballāḷa III died in the battle of Beribi which was actually fought on September 8, 1342.

* *EC.* vi. Cm. 105.

armies were depriving him of his kingdom district by district. An idea of the progress of the Vijayanagara conquest may be had from the following table :—

District.	Reference.	Date of the latest Hoysala inscription.	Reference.	Date of the earliest Vijayanagara inscription.
Anantapūr ...	MER. 102 of 1926-7	1340	LA. I. p. 119-20 Penugoṇḍa No. 23	1344
Citaldrug ...	Cd. 6	1338	Cd. 67	1345
Kōlār ...	Kl. 32	1342	Mb. 158	1343
Bangalore ...	Bn. 41	1343	Nl. 19	1340
Tumkūr ...	Si. 10	1341	Pg. 54	1354
Mysore ...	Hg. 112	1342	Hs. 114	1344
Hāssan ...	Ak. 83	1338	Ak. 159	1343
Kaḍūr ...	Cm. 45	1342	Sg. 1	1346
Ṣīmoga ...	Sb. 494	1334	Sb. 253	1342

The earliest Vijayanagara inscription in the Hoysala kingdom comes from the Bangalore district. Nl. 19 which is dated in 1340 records the grant of a certain *Mahāsāmantādhipati* Mayileya Nāyaka who was ruling Kukkalanāḍ as a subordinate of Harihara I. This chief appears to be a descendant of Mayileya Nāyaka-Cenneya Nāyaka who was ruling in Kukkalanāḍ as a subordinate of Ballāḷa III in 1333.* It is evident that Mayileya Nāyaka transferred his allegiance to the king of Vijayanagara sometime before 1340. Mayileya the ruler of Kukkalanāḍ would not have recognised Harihara I as his overlord, unless he was subjugated by force of arms. It would mean that Harihara invaded the Hoysala kingdom before 1340.

* *EC.* ix. No. 9.

Probably Ballappa Daṇṇāyaka who was guarding, as described already, the eastern frontier, was defeated, and the Vijayanagara forces overran the districts of the Hoysala kingdom in the neighbourhood of the frontier. Their success, however, seems to have been short-lived; for a few of Ballāḷa III's inscriptions dated in the succeeding year are found in the Nelamangala tālūka.

The conquest of the Hoysala kingdom was seriously undertaken in 1343. Kōlār in the east and Hāssan in the west seems to have passed finally into the hands of Harihara I. The coronation of Ballāḷa IV was celebrated on Friday, 5th day of the dark fortnight of of the month of *Śrāvaṇa* in the year *Śvabhānu* corresponding to Śaka 1265.* The first inscription of Harihara is dated on Thursday 1st of the bright half of the month of *Kārttika* in the year *Śvabhānu* corresponding to Śaka 1265.† Therefore, Harihara I wrested from Ballāḷa IV the district of Hāssan in which his capital Dōrasamudra stood within three months after his coronation. Probably Dōrasamudra itself fell into the hands of Harihara at the same time. The conquest of the other districts followed soon. Although 1343 is the latest date found in the Hoysala inscriptions, the earliest of Vijayanagara inscriptions in all the districts do not belong to that year or the next. The earliest date of Vijayanagara grants in Penugoṇḍa, Kōlār and Mysore is 1344; in Citaldrug it is 1345; in Bangalore it is 1340; and in Kaḍūr it is 1346. And no Vijayanagara record belonging to a date prior to 1354 is so far discovered in Tumkūr. It is clear that the conquerors did not find their task easy. They met with resistance from the officers and dependents of the departed Hoysala kings. Nevertheless

* *EC.* vi. Cm. 105.

† *EC.* v. Ak. 159.

they were able to bring under their control most of the Hoysala territory before 1346.

The warfare of these years is also mentioned in the inscriptions of the time :—

Reference.	Date.	Donor.	Object.
EC. x. Mr. 16.	1343	A trustee of the temple of Aruḷāḷanātha Perumāḷ.	"For the success of the sword and arm of Vallappa Daṇṇāyakar."
EC. x. Ct. 82.	1344	Varundaram Perumāḷ.	"For the success of the sword and arm of Bukkarāya."
EC. iv. Hs. 114.	1344	Certain people of the village Capparadahaḷḷi.	Set up a *viragal* in memory of certain *gowḍas* who fell in the service of Hariyappa Voḍeyar.

In addition to these, several explicit references to the conquest of the Hoysala kingdom are met with in the inscriptions of the time of Bukka I. Mallinātha Voḍeya, son of Aḷiya Sāyi Nāyaka, one of the officers of Bukka I secured victories over the Hoysala army. * Tipparāja, another officer, of Bukka captured the fort of Ucchangi. † Tippaṇṇa Voḍeyar with Teppada

* *EC.* xi. Cd. 2, 3.

† *EC.* vi. Mg. 25.

Nāgaṇṇa, the president of Bukka's council, subjugated the Hoysaṇa country. According to the inscription describing this campaign, these officers were unwilling to give up Sosavūr, the birth place of the Hoysalas. Evidently they were besieged in the place by some enemey who pressed them to surrender it; however, as they were confident that they could withstand the besiegers, they expressed their unwillingness to give it up. The idea of surrender could not have arisen, except under circumstances as described above. Now, who could be the enemy that was interested in taking Sosavūr? It is said that the Hoysalas held this place in great veneration, owing to the fact that the family had its origin there. As Sosavūr was not an important place, its possession could have been desired only on sentimental grounds. Therefore, it may reasonably be supposed that the people who pressed for the surrender of Sosavūr were none other than the Hoysalas. It is probably to this campaign that Bukka I refers in one of his inscriptions. "Having freed from enemies one hundred royal cities beginning from Dōrasamudra, he ruled over a kingdom perfect in seven parts." * He is also said to have made the Hoysala kingdom an ornament to his arm, that is, after conquering it. †

The subjugation of nearly the whole of the Hoysala country should have been completed, as already mentioned, before 1346. A few places probably still resisted the officers of Harihara; but their conquest was considered inevitable. Harihara appears to have felt that he should celebrate the completion of the conquest of the country between the two seas in a suitable manner. ‡ Therefore he summoned his brothers, relations, dependents, and officers to Sṛngēri

* *EC.* iv. Yd. 46. † *MAR.* 1925. p. 73. ‡ *EC.* vi Sg. I.

to attend a festival which he wanted to celebrate in honour of his victory; and the festival was accordingly celebrated in 1346 A. D., when liberal gifts were distributed among the assembled Brāhmaṇs. Henceforward, the authority of the Rāyas was firmly established in the Hoysala country, in spite of the outbreak of a few rebellions here and there. *

* There appears to have been some disturbance in the Canarese country at the beginning of the reign of Harihara II. A rebellion broke out in Konkan in 1380. "Some base persons born in the Konkan country, having risen against him, in the war (which followed), Baicappa greatly distinguished himself, sent many of the Konkaṇigas to destruction, and gained the heavenly world." The rebellion seems to have spread to the Hoysala country also; for in an inscription of 1384, (*Jr. Bom. Hist. Soc* i. p. 126) it is said that the Hoysalas were one of the people whom Harihara II had conquered. "Having conquered his enemies, and the prominent countries of kings of Karṇāṭa, Kuntala, Konkaṇa, Hoysala, Āndhra, Pāṇḍya and Cōḷa the great lord of the earth (i e., Harihara II) enjoys all glories." This seems to have been the last effort of the people of the Hoysaṇa country to throw off the yoke of Vijayanagara. Very soon, the authority of the Rāyas became firmly established and the Hoysaṇa country remained under them as long as their power lasted.

APPENDICES

DHĀRWĀR DISTRICT.

Hoysala				Sēuṇa		
Ballāḷa II ...	MER.					
	F 113 of 1926-27	1192 A.D:				
	F 8 of 1926-27	1192				
	F 36 of 1926-27	1193				
	E 57 of 1927-28	1195–6				
	F 189 of 1926-27	1197				
	E 187 of 1928-29	1197				
	F 6 of 1926-27	1199				
	F 153 of 1926-27	1199				
	E 193 of 1928-29	1202				
	F 155 of 1926-27	1205				
	E 191 of 1928-29	1205				
	F 87 of 1926-27	1207–8				
	F 116 of 1926-27	1207–8				
	F 22 of 1926-27	1211				
	F 52 of 1926-27	1212				
	F 142 of 1926-27	—				
	E 195 of 1928-29	—				

		Singhaṇa ...	F 9 of 1926-27	1213
			F 154 of 1926-27	1215
			F 23 of 1926-27	1216
			E 36 of 1927-28	1221
			E 37 of 1927-28	1221
			E 55 of 1927-28	1223
			F 53 of 1926-27	1223–4
			F 96 of 1926-27	1224–5
			E 79 of 1927-28	1226
			F 200 of 1926-27	1230
			E 30 of 1927-28	1232
			F 58 of 1926-27	1236
			F 233 of 1926-27	1242
			F 201 of 1926-27	1243–4
			A 4 of 1925-26	1251
		Kannara ...	F 187 of 1926-27	Nil
			E 200 of 1928-29	„
		Mahādēva ...	Nil	
		Rāmacandra ...	E 66 of 1927-28	1284
			F 159 of 1926-27	1288

ṢĪMOGA DISTRICT.

	Hoysala		Sēuṇa	
Sorab Tālūka :—				
Ballāḷa II ...	Sb 2	1180		
	Sb 419	1183		
	Sb 30	1193		
	Sb 13	1196		
	Sb 98	1196		
	Sb 514	1197		
	Sb 515	1197		
	Sb 140	1198		
	Sb 402	1199		
	Sb 148	1204		
	Sb 332	1205		
	Sb 333	1205		
	Sb 171	1207		
	Sb 28	1208		
	Sb 305	1208		
	Sb 307	1208		
	Sb 377	1209		
	Sb 4	1211		

	Sb 404	1211			
	Sb 376	1212			
	Sb 516	1212			
			Singhaṇa ...	Sb 309	1212
				Sb 276 (iii)	1215
				Sb 391	1216
				Sb 398	1216
				Sb 507	1216
				Sb 135	1217
				Sb 339	1217
				Sb 256	1218
				Sb 423	1218
Narasimha II ...	Nil			Sb 308	1223
				Sb 293	1224
				Sb 275	1231
				Sb 403	1234
Sōmēśwara ...	Sb 492	1239		Sb 269	1235
	Sb 334	1242		Sb 250	1237
				Sb 319	1239

ṢĪMOGA DISTRICT—(*Contd*).

	Hoysala		Sēuṇa		
Sorab Tālūka :— (*Contd.*)					
				Sb 387	1241
				Sb 321	1242
				Sb 425	1242
				Sb 217	1243
				Sb 322	1244
				Sb 427	1248
			Kannara ...	Sb 426	1248
				Sb 340	1249
				Sb 136	1255
			Mahādēva ..	Sb 285	1265 (about)
Narasimha III ...	Nil		Rāmacandra ..	Sb 517	1258
				Sb 137	1272
				Sb 292	1275
				MAR. 1929 No. 69	1276

				Sb 275 (ii)	1280
				Sb 160	1282
				Sb 57	1282
				Sb 189	1283
				Sb 284	1283
				Sb 31	1284
				Sb 34	1284
				Sb 352	1286
				Sb 203	1286
				Sb 93	1288
				Sb 128	1288
				Sb 219	1288
				Sb 247	1288
				Sb 209	1289
				Sb 113	1290
				Sb 192	1290
				Sb 210	1291
				Sb 198	1292
				Sb 502	1294
				Sb 101	1295
				Sb 124	1295
				Sb 298	1300

ṢĪMOGA DISTRICT—(*Contd*).

Hoysala			Sēuṇa		
Ballāḷa III ...	Sb 162 Sb 494	1314 1334			
Sāgar Tālūka :—					
Ballāḷa II ...	Sa 4 Sa 15	1193 1218	Singhaṇa ...	MAR. 1928 No. 69	Nil
Narasimha II ...	Sa 126	1226			
Sōmēśwara ...	Nil		Kannara ...	Sa 119	1250 (about)
Narasimha III ...	Nil		Mahādēva ...	Sa 137	1270
			Rāmacandra ...	Sa 69 & 70 Sa 86 Sa 63	1276 1282 1283

Ballāḷa III ...	Sa 96	1299			
	Sa 98	1299			
	Sa 45	1300			
	Sa 101	1303			
	Sa 156	1305			
	Sa 62	1307			
	Sa 135	1320			
	Sa 104	1329			
Ṣikārpūr Tālūka :–					
Ballāḷa II ...	Sk 212	1181	Singhaṇa ...		
	Sk 168	1182			
	Sk 145	1184			
	Sk 143	1186			
	Sk 148	1186			
	Sk 214	1186			
	Sk 105	1193			
	Sk 138	1194			
	Sk 315	1198			
	Sk 186	1200			
	Sk 156	1202			
	Sk 113	1203			

ṢĪMOGA DISTRICT—(*Contd*).

Hoysala			Sēuṇa		
Sikārpūr Tālūka :- (*Contd*).					
Ballāḷa II-(*Contd*).	Sk 244	1203	Singhaṇa ...		
	Sk 225	1204			
	Sk 235 (a)	1207			
	Sk 235 (b)	1209			
	Sk 202	1211			
	Sk 196	1212			
	Sk 247	1215			
				Sk 243	1214
				Sk 95	1215
				MAR. 1928 No. 74	1217 (about)
Narasimha II ...	Nil			Sk 270	1222
				Sk 273	1222
				Sk 175	1223
				Sk 268	1223
				Sk 248	1224
				Sk 274	1230

				Sk 80	1244 ?
Sōmēśwara ...	Nil		Kannara ...	Sk 217	1248
				Sk 198	1256
				Sk 199	1256
				Sk 271	1256
			Mahādēva ...	Sk 41	1268
Narasimha III ...	Nil		Rāmacandra.	MAR 1923 No. 61	1282
				MAR 1928 No. 75	1282
				Sk 203	1283
				Sk 122	1284
				Sk 140	1284
				Sk 141	1286
Ballāḷa III ...	Nil			Sk 211	1294
				MAR 1929 No. 57	1294–5
Hannaḷi Tālūka:—					
Ballāḷa II ...	Hl 45	1175			
	Hl 91	1185			
	Hl 111	1185			
	Hl 108	1203			
	Hl 7	1204			

ṢĪMOGA DISTRICT.—(*Contd.*)

Hoysala.			Sēuṇa.		
			Honali Tālūka:—		
			Singhaṇa ...	Hl 44	1215
				Hl 48	1216
				Hl 20	1222
				Hl 43	1232
Narasimha II ...	Hl 8	1228	Kannara ...	Nil	
Sōmēśwara ...	Nil		Mahādēva ...	Nil	
Narasimha III ...	Hl 11	1289	Rāmacandra ...	Hl 17	1286
	Hl 90	1290		Hl 18	1286
				Hl 29	1294
Ballāḷa III ...	Hl 76	1314			
	Hl 117	1319			

Cannagiri Tālūka :—					
Ballāḷa II ...	Ci 73	1180			
	Ci 77	1180			
	Ci 37	1200			
	Ci 64	1214			
	Ci 6	1220			
Narasimha II ...	Ci 45	1229	Singhaṇa ..	Nil	
	Ci 52	1233			
			Kannara ...	Nil	
Sōmēśwara ...	Nil		Mahādēva ...	Ci 4	1265
Narasimha III ...	Nil			Ci 21	1268
				Ci 22	1268
Ballāḷa III ...	Ci 65	1340	Rāmacandra ...	Ci 2	1277
				Ci 24	1280
				Ci 23	1282
				Ci 26	1295

CITALDRUG DISTRICT.

Hoysala			Sēuṇa		
Dāvaṇagere Tālūka :—					
Ballāḷa II ...	Dg 105	1218	Singhaṇa ...	Nil	
Narasimha II ...	Dg 69	1220			
	Dg 25	1224			
			Kannara ...	Dg 88	1250
Sōmēśwara ...	Dg 129	1236		Dg 50	1254
				Dg 103	1258
				Dg 48	1263
Narasimha III ..	Dg 36	1268	Mahādēva ...	Dg 87	1264
	Dg 132	1280		Dg 97	1264
	Dg 137	1283		Dg 8	1265
				Dg 100	1265
				Dg 162	1265
				Dg 163	1265
				Dg 171	1266
				Dg 172	1266
				Dg 79	1268

Ballāḷa III ...	Nil		Rāmacandra ...	Dg 13	1271
				Dg 70 (a)	1275
				Dg 70 (b)	1276
				Dg 59	1280
				Dg 81	1288
				Dg 26	1300
Halāḷkere Tālūka :—					
			Kannara ...	Hk 36	1263
Jagaḷūru Tālūka :-					
			Rāmacandra ...	Jl 30	1279

APPENDIX B.

NOTE ON DORAVADI.

(*a*) The Sources:—The following account of Doravadi is based upon eleven inscriptions whose dates range from A. D. 1280 to A. D. 1325. These inscriptions are here given in a schedule for the convenience of reference:—

Reference.	Date.	The place of residence of Kampila or his father.	Information contained in the inscription.
EC. VII. Ci. 24.	1280	Doravadi.	Cauṇḍarasa, a subordinate of Rāmacandra of Dēvagiri in Kurugōḍu nāḍu, marched to Doravadi against Mummaḍi Singeya Nāyaka, but was slain in battle.
EC. XI. Hr. 86.	1281-2	...	Mummaḍi Singeya Nāyaka marched upon a place the name of which ends with .... mmalūrakallu, and laid siege to it.
EC. XI. Hr. 37.	do.	...	Mummaḍi Singeya Nāyaka fought against a chief called Singeya Nāyaka at Vetaṇḍakal.

Reference.	Date.	The place of residence of Kampila or his father.	Information contained in the inscription.
EC. XI. DG. 26.	1300	...	Khandeyarāya, son of Mummaḍi Singeya Nāyaka restored to Brāhmaṇs the *agrahāra* of Harihara.
MAR. 1913 P. 50.	1303	...	Kampiladēva, the general of the army of Rāmacandra of Dēvagiri, marched against Holāḷkere, and killed in battle, Ballāḷa III's brother-in-law, Sōmeya Daṇṇāyaka who was governing the fort of Bemmattanakallu.
EC. XI. Hr. 106.	1303	...	Kampiladēva marched upon Holāḷkere and fought with Ballāḷa's subordinates. Sōmeya Daṇṇāyaka of Bemmattanakallu fought with Kampila, when Sāyaṇṇa the betel-bearer of Sōmeya was killed.
LR. 46. (Hampe) VR. Ap 335	1309	...	Vīra Kampiladēva, son of Mummaḍi Singeya Nāyaka built a temple at Hampi, dedicated to Prasanna Virūpākṣa.

Reference.	Date.	The place of residence of Kampila or his father.	Information contained in the inscription.
EC. VIII. Nr. 19.	1320	Doravadi.	Ballāḷa III marched with all his forces to Doravadi, against Vīra Kampiladēva. A battle was fought, and probably Ballāḷa was defeated.
EC. XII TP. 24.	1325		A damaged inscription. Refers to the war between Ballāḷa III, and Kampiladēva. Refers to the death of some person.
MAR. 1923 No. 121.	Nil	Siruguppe.	Ballāḷa III invaded the kingdom of Vīra-Kampiladēva, and lay encamped at Siruguppe. A battle was fought in which some of Ballāḷa's officers were killed. The inscription is only a fragment.

(*b*) The extent of the kingdom — EC. VII Ci. 24 mentions Doravadi in Kurugōḍu nāḍu as the place of Mummaḍi Singeya Nāyaka's residence; his dominions extended in the south as far as Holāḷkere in the Citaldrug district. (EC XI. Hr. 106; MAR 1912,

p. 45; MAR 1913; p. 50). It included Harihara and probably also the whole of Dāvaṇagere tālūka. (EC. XI. Dg. 26). In the east, it extended as far as Siruguppe in the Beḷḷāry district (MAR. 1923 No. 121). So far as can be deduced from these inscriptions, the kingdom of Kampiladēva comprised large portions of the present Beḷḷāry and Citaldrug districts.

(*c*) Doravadi :—Where was Doravadi situated? According to EC. VII. Ci. 24 it was included in the Kurugōḍu nāḍu. Where was Kurugōḍu nāḍu? The district was evidently named after its chief town Kurugōḍu, which is identical with the present Kurugōḍu in the Beḷḷāry tālūka. Therefore, the town, Doravadi should be looked for in the Beḷḷāry tālūka or somewhere in its neighbourhood. An inscription of a subordinate of the Sinda chief, Kalidēva of Kurugōḍu, limits the field of our search further.

ವಾರಾಶಿಪರೀತೋರ್ವ್ಯುದ್ಧಾರಣಿ ಮಧ್ಯಮೆನಿಸೆಸೆವಮೇರುವತೆಂಕಲ್
ರಾರಾಜಿಪಕುಂತಳ ಧರೆಗೋರನ್ತಿರಬಲ್ಲಕುಂದಿ ನಾಡೆಸೆದಿರ್ಕ್ಕುಂ ||
ಆನಾಳ್ಕೆಪಟ್ಟಣಂ ಲಕ್ಷ್ಮೀನಿಳಯಂ ತಾನೆನಿಪ್ಪಕುರುಗೋಡವನು
ವೀರನುತಕಲಿದೇವ ನೃಪಂ ತಾನೊಲವಿಂ ಪಾಳಿಸುತ್ತಿರೆಪಣಿವಂಶಂ ||
ಫಳಿತಸುರಕುಜದಚೆಲ್ವಂ ತಳೆದಿರ್ದಾಬಲ್ಲಕುಂದೆ ನಾಡೊಳ್ತೊಳ್ತೋಂ
ದೆಳ್ಗೊಂಚಿನದೊರವದಿ ನಾಡೆಳೆಯೊಳ್ ರಂಜಿಪ್ಪುದುನೋಡೆನಾಡುಗಳರಸಂ ||
ಆದೊರವಡಿನಾಡೊಳ್ಪಂ ಪಾತೀರ್ಥಮಿಪ್ಪುದದೆನ್ತನೆ ||

SII. iv. 260.

From this, it is seen that Doravadi nāḍu was in Ballakunde 300, of which the capital was the town of Kurugōḍu. What is more interesting still is that Hampe was included in the district of Doravadi. As Ballakunde was a small district, the town of Doravadi must have stood somewhere in the neighbourhood of Hampe. No place of the name seems to exist at present in the Hospēṭ tālūka in which Hampe is included, or anywhere else in the Beḷḷāry district as to that matter.

There is, however, a place called Darōji in the neighbourhood of Hampe, and it is not unlikely that it represents the old town of Doravadi. This is not a wild guess. An inscription from Kurukuppe very near Darōji (MER. 727 of 1922) refers 'to a temple of Virūpākṣa built at Kureya-kuppe an *agrahāra* village in the Doravadi *venṭhe* of the Hastināvati *vaḷita*. Therefore, Darōji may be taken as the modern name of the ancient Doravadi.

If Darōji (Doravadi) were the place of residence of Kampiladēva, then Hampe which is almost within a dozen miles of Darōji, should have been included in his kingdom. This is proved by an epigraph of Vīra Kampiladēva at Hampe recording the construction of the temple of Prasanna Virūpākṣa in 1309. Therefore, Ballāḷa III who was in a chronic state of war with Kampiladēva could not have secured a footing so very close to the latter's capital as Hampe; nor could he have built any fort or city in the place. After the death of Kampiladēva, his kingdom was annexed by the Sultān of Delhi who entrusted its government about 1336 to Harihara I of Vijayanagara. It is pretty certain that Ballāḷa III had nothing to do with the construction of the city of Vijayanagara.

(*d*) *Relations with the Kākatīyas*:—The position of the kingdom of Doravadi, situated as it was between the Hoysala and the Kākatīya dominions brought it often into hostile contact with its neighbours. The wars which Kampiladēva waged with Ballāḷa III have been already described in the body of the present work. An attempt is here made to narrate briefly Kampiladēva's relations with the Kākatīya king. It is stated in *the Bhīmēśvarapurāṇa* of Śrīnātha that Prōlaya Anna, one of the generals of Pratāparudra II destroyed the pleasure gardens of Kummaṭa. * The battle, in which the early Āravīṭi chief, Kōṭikanṭi Rāghava defeated Kampiladēva, was probably fought in the course of this invasion. † The cause of this struggle is not very difficult to find. Almost the whole of the western Telugu country was included in the Sēuṇa dominions during the reigns of Singhaṇa and Kannara. Their inscriptions are found as far south-east as Jammalamaḍugu in the Cuddapah district. The Sēuṇa authority in the Telugu country was gradually overthrown by the Kākatīyas. The country corresponding to the present districts of Cuddapah and Kurnool was conquered by Gaṇapati; but a portion of the Telugu country was still left in the hands of the Sēuṇas. During the early years of Pratāparudra II, a successful attempt was made to wrest the remaining Telugu districts from Rāmadēva. Viṭṭhala-bhūnātha, one of the generals serving under Pratāparudra marched probably

* వీరరుద్రాశేవ విశ్వంభరాధీశ పృథుల దక్షిణ భుజాపీఠ మనఁగ
తే. యవన సంహార విలయకాలాగ్నియనఁగ
ధాటివిఘటిత కుమ్మఠోద్యానుఁ డనఁగ
విశ్వలోక ప్రశస్తుఁడై వినుతికెక్కె
నతుల బలిసీరిపోలయ యన్నశౌరి ॥

Bhimēśvarapurāṇam. 1: 48.

† విరుదాంచితుఁడు తాత పిన్న భూవరుఁడు
పారికాంతబోలు సూరాంబికయందు
ఘనశౌర్యుఁడా కోటికంటి రాఘవుని
గనియెనతండు సంగ్రామంబు నందు
రాజిల్లు కంపిలిరాయ సైన్యములఁ
దేజంబు మెఱయంగఁ దెగువమై గెలిచి
గరిమె గైకొనెను నగ్గండరగూళి
విరుదంబు నరినృపుల్ పేర్కొని పొగడ.

Bālabhāgavatam : *The Bhārati.* vi. p. 848.

from Pānugal at the head of his army, and "captured the forts of Ādavani, Tumbuḷam, Mānuva and Hāluva." He entered the fort of Rāicūr in A. D. 1295, and constructed a 'stone fort (in the place of a mud one) for the protection of all the kingdom and the people.' * As a result of Viṭṭhala's conquests, the western boundary of the Kākatīya kingdom passed very near Kampili, the most important city in Kampiladēva's dominions. The expansion of his kingdom towards the west should have brought Pratāparudra II into violent contact with Kampila, who seems to have suffered defeat in the struggle that followed. But the history of this struggle still remains obscure ; and it is not possible, at the present state of our knowledge, to describe fully all the events connected with it.

* *ASPP.* vi. pp. 36-38 ; *MAR.* 1907, p. 14.

Appendix C.

A NOTE ON KANYA NĀYAK. *

The name of the Hindu leader who successfully headed the rebellion in Telingāṇa against Sultān Muhammad in 1344 is given differently by the Muhammadan historians. Zia Barnī refers to him as Kanya Nāyak; Nizam-ud-Din Ahmad calls him Kanya-pāik; and Ferishta speaks of him as Kṛṣṇ Nāyak. The name of the leader is made up of two words: (1) Kanya or Kṛṣṇa (2) Nāyak or pāik. So far as the first part of the name is concerned, it may be said that there is no real difference; for, the word Kanya is but the Telugu form of the Prākṛt Kaṇha which is derived from the Sānskṛt Kṛṣṇa. Therefore, the words Kṛṣṇa and Kanya must be taken as identical. The same thing, however, cannot be said of the second part, the words '*nāyak*' and '*pāik*' being radically different in their origin and meaning. *Nāyak* means a chief, or leader, and *pāik* has no intelligible meaning either in Telugu or Sānskṛt.

Syed Ali Azīz-ul-la Tabātaba, the author of *Burhān-i-ma'asir* spells the word differently, though it is not easy to discover how exactly he originally spelt it. In one manuscript, i. e., the one adopted by Major King as the text of his translation, the word is written as Kanā-bāyand; but in the manuscript

* M. S. Śarma, in an interesting article contributed to the *JAHS*. v. pp. 217-32, arrives at the same conclusion, though he approaches the problem from a different standpoint.

preserved in the British Museum, this name is written in one place as Kabā-nand, and in another place as Kanā-nīdah. Even in Major King's text the spelling of the word is not uniformly the same, for, it is written in one place without any dot to the second letter in order to indicate its phonetic value. * The *Burhān-i-ma'asir*, therefore, gives four different forms of the name :—

کنابایند
کباتند
کنانیده
کٮابایند

The last may be left out of account, as it is not possible to read it in the absence of the dot to indicate the phonetic value of the second letter. The remaining three forms are Kanā-bāyand, Kabā-nand, and Kanā-nīdah. The name here also contains two members (i) Kanā or Kabā and (ii) bāyand, nand, or nīdah. Kanā, no doubt, is the same word as Kanya; and *nand* or *nīdah* appears to be a corruption of *nāyaḍu*, *nāyaṇḍu*, *nīḍu*, all meaning a *nāyak* or chief; but Kabā and *bāyand* still remain unexplained like the *pāik* of Nizam-ud-Din Ahmad. In fact, there seems to be something in common between Syed Ali and Nizam-ud-Din. One of the forms which the name assumes in *Burhān-i-ma'asir* is Kanā-bāyand. Let us compare it with Kanya-pāik. They are the same. The word *bāyand* like *pāik* gives no sense. We know from Barnī that the right word is '*nāyak*', and not '*pāik.*' How did the 'p' displace the 'n' in the text of Nizam-ud-Din?

* *IA.* xxviii. p. 145 n. 15, p. 146 n. 16.

The word Kabā, suggests the clue. Suppose we interchange the place of 'n' in 'Kanya' with that of 'p' in '*pāik*', we get 'Kapya-nāyak' in the place of Kanya-pāik. If we adopt the spelling of *Burhān-i-ma'asir*, we should write the name as 'Kapya-nāyand,' which closely resembles Kabā-nand, one of the forms of the name given in that book. We believe that the real name of the leader of Telingāṇa who revolted against Sultān Muhammad is Kapya-nāyand (Kāpaya Nāyaṇḍu), and not Kanya or Kṛṣṇa Nāyaka. Our belief is based upon the following facts.

Kanya Nāyak according to the Mussalman historians rose up in rebellion at Warrangal in 1344; and he ruled Telingāṇa with Warrangal as his capital until at least 1365 A. D. He was an enemy of Sultān Alā-ud-Din Bahmani I and of his son Muhammad Shah with whom he fought several battles. It is evident from this that Kanya Nāyak was a great leader of the Telingāṇa Hindus; and that he re-established the lost independence of Telingāṇa, and maintained it successfully for thirty years. He should have left some records behind him to perpetuate his name and fame. Have we got any of his records?

When we search the Hindu records of the time, *viz.*, the inscriptions, we find that Warrangal and with it Telingāṇa was really in the possession of a Hindu king between 1346 and 1360; his name, however, was not Kanya Nāyak but Kāpaya Nāyaka. He was ruling Āndhradēśa probably from Warrangal, and fought with the Sultān Alā-ud-Din I of Gulburga. He seems to have several things in common with Kanya Nāyak.

Kāpaya Nāyaka.	Kanya Nāyak.
1. He was *Āndhradēśādhīśvara* or *Āndhra Suratrāṇa.* *	1. He was *Wali* or the ruler of Telingāṇa.
2. His capital was probably Warrangal.	2. His capital was Warrangal.
3. His first inscription is dated in 1346; † and his latest is dated in 1360. ‡	3. He became the ruler of Warrangal in 1344 and was ruling in 1365.
4. He was an enemy of Sultān Alā-ud-Din I of Gulburga with whom he fought. §	4. He was an enemy of the Sultāns Alā-ud-Din I and Muhammad Shah of Gulburga with whom he fought several times.

The facts stated in the foregoing table make it clear that Kāpaya Nāyaka and Kanya Nāyak were holding sway over Telingāṇa at the same time, having probably the same city of Warrangal as their capital. Moreover, both of them fought against the same enemy, the Sultān Alā-ud-din I of Gulburga. Therefore, Kāpaya and Kanya appear to be the names of the same person.

If the real name of the leader of the Telingāṇa rebellion was Kāpaya Nāyaḍu, how did he come to be known as Kanya Nāyak to the Mussalman historians? It is easily explained: as *nāyak*, *nāyaḍu*, and

* *SII.* fv. 950. † *ibid.* ‡ *ibid.* vi. 821.

§ *Telingāṇa inscriptions*: Miscellaneous 11.

nāyaṇḍu are but different forms of the same word, they do not need an explanation. The real difficulty is about the term Kāpaya. How did it assume the form Kanya? The word Kabā of *Burhān-i-ma'asir* must be taken into consideration in this context. Kāpaya was at first transformed into Kabaya and then to Kabā. In the Persian language the letters پ and ب are interchangeable. Very often the same word is spelt with a پ or ب according to the whim of the writer or caligraphist. A few examples are sufficient to illustrate the point. '*Asp*' اسپ in Persian means a horse; but the word is also written as اسب '*asb*'; the term '*pādshāh*' is written both as پادشاه and بادشاه; and Dīpālpūr (the name of a city in Hindūstān) is spelt in two ways: دیپالپور and دیبالپور. Examples can easily be multiplied; but these are enough. The word Dīpālpūr is of special interest in this context. It is an Indian term, denoting the name of a city. In spite of it, its spelling had undergone a change in the hands of the Persian writers. Similarly the name of Kāpaya was transformed into Kabaya or Kabā; and this form, as we have already noticed, is preserved in one of the manuscripts of the *Burhān-i-ma'asir*. The transformation of Kabā into Kanā may be explained in two ways. A careless scribe might have placed the dot above the letter instead of below, then کبا would become کنا; or the change might be attributed to metathesis. Nizam-ud-Din Ahmad calls the leader of Telingāṇa rebellion Kanya-pāik instead of Kanya Nāyak like other writers. This form of the name is also preserved in one of the manuscripts of *Burhān-i-ma'asir*. The text of Major King spells the name as Kanā-bāyand. Therefore, the name Kāpaya Nāyaḍu became Kanya Nāyak, as a consequence of a double transformation at the hands of the Persian writers.

Was this Kāpaya or Kanya Nāyak, a son of Pratāparudra II of Warrangal? The answer to this question is in the negative. The Hindu records mention a son of Pratāparudra, but he was known as Vīrabhadra.* A certain Juṭṭaya-*lenka* Gonkā Reḍḍi is also spoken of by several writers as one of Pratāparudra's sons; but this is a mistake. Juṭṭaya, as the term '*lenka*' indicates, was a servant and not the son of Pratāparudra. Kāpaya Nāyaka whom we have identified with Kanya Nāyak had no connection whatever with Pratāparudra. In fact, the statement of Ferishta that Kṛṣṇa (Kanya) Nāyak was a son of Pratāparudra is not supported by evidence. Neither Barnī nor Nizam-ud-Din mention that Kanya Nāyak was Pratāparudra's son. On the contrary, they seem to indicate that he was one of the zamindars of Telingāṇa. That is the truth. It is not possible to know the source from which Ferishta obtained his inaccurate information.

* Ekāmranātha: *Pratāpacaritra* pp. 79-80.

Appendix D.

KARṆĀṬA AND ĀNDHRA.

Some writers believe that the founders of Vijayanagara could not be the members of a Telugu family as Bukka I and Harihara II claim victories over the Āndhras. But this view is due to the misconception that the terms Karṇāṭa and Āndhra respectively denoted in those days the areas over which the Kannaḍa and the Telugu languages are now spoken. This is far from the truth. During the fourteenth and the fifteenth centuries, nearly one third of the land inhabited by the Telugu speaking people was known as Karṇāṭa. The Telugu poet Śrīnātha who was a contemporary of Harihara II, Dēvarāya I, and Dēvarāya II, declares that the language of his poems is *Karṇāṭa-bhāṣā*. "Sanskrit is said to be most suited for dignified composition, and Āndhra for witty expression. Whatever critics may say, I do not mind: certain it is that my poetry is written in the Karṇāṭa language." * At first sight it may appear that the *Karṇāṭa-bhāṣā* in which Śrīnātha claims to have written his poems is the Kanarese language; but all the works of Śrīnātha are written in Telugu, and there is no reason to believe that he knew Kanarese, for which he had little love. †

What then is the meaning of Śrīnātha's statement? Although it looks very enigmatic to the people of the

* ప్రౌఢి బలికింప సంస్కృతభాష యండ్రు
పలుకునుడికారమున కాంధ్రభాష యండ్రు
యెవ్వరేమన్నగాని నాకేమి కొదువ
నాకవిత్వంబు నిజము కర్ణాటభాష॥.

Bhīmēśvarapurāṇam, 1: 15.

† cf. 'అస్తావిస్తపుఁ గన్నడంబు'

Cāṭupadyamaṇimañjari, I. p. 128.

present age, his contemporaries could not have entertained any doubts. They knew that he wrote in the idiom of his native district, Pākanāḍu which was included in the Karṇāṭa country. It was only natural that a poet who proudly styled himself as "the sun to the lotus garden viz., the cities of Karṇāṭa," * should have chosen the language of that country as the medium to express his thoughts. It is evident from this that Nellore and the eastern part of Cuddapah which correspond to ancient Pākanāḍu were known as Karṇaṭa during the time of Śrīnātha. This is confirmed by other writers. The poet Tripurāntaka, the grandfather of Ayyalarāju Rāmabhadra who lived in the court of Kṛṣṇadēva Rāya, refers to the god Raghuvīra of Onṭimiṭṭa in the Cuddapah district as "the lord of Karṇāṭa." † The evidence of literature is corroborated by an inscription coming from the Ongōle tālūka of the Gunṭūr district dated A.D. 1441. According to this record, the town of Udayagiri is said to be in the middle of Karṇāṭa: "*Udayagiryākhya nagarē kāntē Karṇāṭakaṭaka madhyasthē.*" ‡ Udayagiri is included in the present Nellore district, and it formed part of ancient Pākanāḍu. It may, therefore, be concluded that during the time of the early Vijayanagara kings, the country comprising the present Nellore and Cuddapah districts was also known as Karṇāṭa. The tradition of the dispute

* కర్ణాటదేశకటక పద్మవనహేళి శ్రీనాథభట్టకవిని.

Kāśikhaṇḍam 1: 7.

† కోటం బీటి నసేక జన్మములనుండిన్ నన్ను వెంటాడుచున్
వాటంబై చనుదెంచు పాపముల శ్రీవత్సాంకనీ వంకనీ
పాటల్ పాడను జేయువారికి మతిస్వాస్థ్యంబుల నాభ్రుకర్
ణ్ణాటాధీశ్వరయొంటిమిట్టరఘువీరా జానకీనాయకా ॥

Śatakamañjari: (Āndhra Grantha Māla I.) p. 71.

‡ *ND.* I, iii. O. 72.

between Śrīnātha and the *pandits* of Rājahmundry over the diction of his poems also supports the view that he employed a local dialect in his works, and called it *Karṇāṭa-bhāṣā* * Consequently the Āndhras whom Bukka I and Harihara II conquered must be people living outside this area.

Who were they? A study of the inscriptions of the Reḍḍis of Koṇḍavīḍu may throw some light upon their identity. In one of the inscriptions of Prōlaya Vēma † dated A. D. 1355 it is said that he was to " the proud Āndhras like the flood of a river washing away the trees " on the banks. This seems to indicate that Vēma waged some wars against the Āndhras. According to an inscription dated 1415 A. D., *Āndhrēśvara* was one of the servants of Tippa, a nephew of Peda-Kōmaṭi Vēma. ‡ Since these Reḍḍis who were Telugus by birth refer to Āndhras as their enemies they should be regarded as the inhabitants of a particular part of the land where Telugu language is spoken.

Now, Kṛṣṇa or Kāpaya Nāyaka who was ruling in Telingāṇa with the city of Warrangal as his capital is referred to in his inscriptions as *Āndhradēśādhīśvara* and *Āndhra Suratrāṇa*. As he was a friend of the kings of Vijayanagara, he could not be the Āndhra

* ... ... ఏ

ద్వ్యంసుల్ రాజమహేంద్ర పట్టణమునన్ ధర్మాసనంబుండి ప్ర
ధ్వంసాభావము ప్రౌఢభావ మనుచున్ చింతింతు రప్రాంతమున్

cf. Vīrabadhra Row, *HA*. iii. p. 216.

As the verse ప్రౌఢిఁబలికింప &c. comes immediately after his disdainful reference to *Kukavis*, this verse should be taken as his defiant declaration that, say what they might, he would still adhere to his own method of composition.

† *ND*. I, iii. O. 73.

‡ *LR*. 42. pp. 243-250.

king whom they conquered. There is no evidence to show that the Reḍḍis of Koṇḍavīḍu had any quarrel with him. However, the Velamas of Rācakoṇḍa, who killed Kāpaya, not only occupied his dominions but appropriated his titles. Henceforward, they were known as *Āndhradēśādhīśvara* and *Āndhra Suratrāṇa*. It is well-known that the Velamas were engaged constantly in warfare with the Reḍḍis on one side, and the kings of Vijayanagara on the other. It is not unlikely that they were the Āndhras who were alluded to in the early Vijayanagara and Reḍḍi inscriptions.

Appendix E.

VIDYĀNAGARA.

In the opinion of some writers, the city of Vijayanagara, was not known by its other name Vidyānagara from the beginning. It is contended that the name was applied to it subsequent to the fall of the Sangama dynasty, on account of the extraordinary influence exercised by the pontiffs of Sṛṅgēri Maṭha over the kings of Vijayanagara. The evidence of all the inscriptions of the first dynasty which mention Vidyānagara has been set aside, as these inscriptions are considered forgeries. Therefore, it has become necessary to search the contemporary literature to find whether the city was referred to as Vidyānagara by any author of the time. So far only two authors are discovered who refer to Vidyānagara, and a careful examination of the books of the period may reveal more. One of the two writers who speak of Vidyānagara is Kallanātha whose evidence has already been considered in the body of the present book. The other is Mallinātha, the famous commentator, who, at the instance of Prauḍha Dēva Rāya wrote a book called the *Vaiśyavamśa-sudhārṇavam*, in order to define the term Vaiśya. The following passage from that book is of interest :

. . . . वाणिज्यनैर्जात्या विवदमानयोः । विवादशांत्यर्थं । कांचि-
स्थशासनोक्तप्रकारेण वैश्यशब्दाभिधेयत्वनागरवैश्यनगरेश्वरदेवतोपास-
कत्वम् तृतीय जातीयत्वम् । कांचिस्थलशासने यस्य प्रवर्तते । तस्य
भवतु नेतरस्येति । श्रीमद्राजाधिराज राजपरमेश्वर श्रीवीरप्रतापप्रौढ-
देवमहारायेण विज्ञापितम् । आज्ञापनानन्तरं तच्छासनमानीय दृष्टम् ।
तद्दृष्टान्तेनैव विद्यानगर धर्मासनप्रकारोऽयम् । यस्तु वैश्यः . . . .

It is evident from this that during the time of Prauḍha Dēva Rāya the city of Vijayanagara was also known as Vidyānagara. Who was this Prauḍha Dēva Rāya? He is generally taken to be Dēvarāya II who ruled at Vijayanagara from 1423 to 1447-8. This, however, is doubtful, as Dēvarāya I is also referred to by this name in some of his inscriptions. * Now, which of these two was the Prauḍha Dēva Rāya who commanded Mallinātha to write the *Vaiśyavamśa-sudhārṇavam*? This can be decided only by discovering the date of Mallinātha. Venkaṭanārāyaṇa, one of his descendants, mentions in his commentary on *Campūrāmāyaṇa* some historical events in connection with the lives of his ancestors, which enable us to fix the date of Mallinātha with tolerable certainty. What he says in brief is this: In the Kōlacalma family, was born Mallinātha the famous *Satāvadhāni* whom Vīra Rudra bathed in a shower of gold; his son was Kapardin, the author of a *kārikā* on the *Śrauta sūtras*; his eldest son was Mallinātha who was remarkable for his intelligence; his younger brother was the great Peddibhaṭṭa who became famous as *Mahōpādhyāya* in all the countries. In a sacrifice performed by his uncle he was bathed in a shower of gold by Sarvajña; he wrote commentaries on several works such as the *Naiṣadha*, *Jyotiṣa*, etc. His son was Kumārasvāmin, the author of a commentary on the *Pratāparudrayaśōbhūṣaṇam*. † The genealogy that is given by Venkaṭanārāyaṇa seems to be faulty in one respect. According to Kumārasvāmin, Peddibhaṭṭa was not an younger brother of Mallinātha, but his son; and Kumārasvāmin was the younger brother of Peddibhaṭṭa who is said to have commented on all *śāstras*. ‡ The genealogy

* *MER*. 399 of 1226.

† *Des. Cat. San. Mss.* (Mad. Govt. Or. Mss. Lib.) xxi pp. 8212-13.

‡ *Pratāparudrayaśōbhūṣaṇam*. (B.S.S.) pp. 1-2.

given by Kumārasvāmin should be accepted as more trustworthy, as he should have known who his father and elder brother were.

If, subject to this correction, the information furnished by Veṅkaṭanārāyaṇa be accepted as genuine, it must be admitted that Mallinātha II, the famous commentator, should have lived in the interval between Pratāparudra II and Sarvajña. As the age of Mallinātha II was nearer to Sarvajña than Pratāparudra, the reign of Sarvajña may be taken as a starting point. Sarvajña was the title conferred upon Singama III, the king of Rācakoṇḍa, by his contemporaries who admired his scholarship. And he appears to have ascended the throne about A. D. 1420.

The Telugu poet Śrīnātha paid a visit to the court of this king while he was still in the service of the Reḍḍis of Koṇḍavīḍu. On this occasion he praised the greatness of Singama, thus in a verse: "The name of Sarvajña can only be given with propriety to Śiva and king Rāvu Singa. To call another Sarvajña is to mistake a dog for an elephant." When Śrīnātha returned to Koṇḍavīḍu, he was obliged to give an explanation for having praised Rāvu Singa, who was an enemy of the Reḍḍis of Koṇḍavīḍu. Śrīnātha is said to have given complete satisfaction to his employers by interpreting the verse in a different manner. "The name Sarvajña can be applied only to Śiva; and Rāvu Singa can have no claim to it. To call any one (excepting Śiva) Sarvajña is to call a dog an elephant."

It is evident from this that at the time of Śrīnātha's visit to Rāvu Singa, the kingdom of Koṇḍavīḍu which was overthrown about A. D. 1420 was still in existence. Śrīnātha's visit to Rācakoṇḍa should have taken place a little earlier; probably he visited Rācakoṇḍa, when he was sent by Peda Kōmaṭi Vēma or his successor to Dēvarakoṇḍa to fetch the Reḍḍi sword called *Nandi-kanta-pōtu-rāju* which had been carried away as a trophy by Mādaya-Linga who defeated the Reḍḍis. Therefore, Sarvajña Singa should have been ruling at Rācakoṇḍa about 1420 A.D.

Peddibhaṭṭa who was bathed in a shower of gold by Sarvajña should have been his contemporary. In that case, Mallinātha II who was the father of Peddibhaṭṭa, must have belonged to the generation before 1420. The king who then ruled at Vijayanagara was Dēvarāya I, and not Dēvarāya II. Therefore it should have been at the instance of Dēvarāya I that Mallinātha composed his *Vaiśyavamśa-sudhārṇavam.*

It is evident from the above discussion that Vijayanagara was also known as Vidyānagara, some seventy years after the foundation of the city. Though we have yet no proof of it, the name might have been in vogue from the time of the foundation of the city.

INDEX

INDEX

INDEX

S

T

U

V

INDEX